Differentiating Instruction With Menus

for the Inclusive Classroom

Math

LOWER & ON-LEVEL MENUS
GRADES 3–5

Differentiating Instruction With Menus

for the Inclusive Classroom

Math

Laurie E. Westphal

Routledge
Taylor & Francis Group

NEW YORK AND LONDON

First published in 2012 by Prufrock Press Inc.

Published 2021 by Routledge
605 Third Avenue, New York, NY 10017
2 Park Square, Milton Park, Abingdon, Oxon OX14 4RN

Routledge is an imprint of the Taylor & Francis Group, an informa business

Library of Congress Cataloging-in-Publication Data

Westphal, Laurie E., 1967-
  Differentiating instruction with menus for the inclusive classroom. Math, grades 3-5 / by Laurie E. Westphal.
    p. cm.
  Includes bibliographical references.
  ISBN 978-1-59363-886-3 (pbk.)
  1. Mathematics--Study and teaching (Elementary) 2. Individualized instruction. 3. Inclusive education. 4. Mixed ability grouping in education. I. Title.

  QA135.6.W474 2012
  372.7--dc23

                      2011050399

ISBN 13: 978-1-0321-4268-5 (hbk)
ISBN 13: 978-1-5936-3886-3 (pbk)

DOI: 10.4324/9781003234241

Printed and bound by CPI Group (UK) Ltd, Croydon, CR0 4YY

CONTENTS

Author's Note

If you are familiar with books on various differentiation strategies, you probably know about the Differentiating Instruction With Menus series. You may be flipping through this book and wondering how this series differs from that series, as well as whether you need to purchase a book from that series in order to use a book from this one. In fact, when we first discussed adding this series to the menu product line, my editor wondered how this new series could be designed so that the two series wouldn't "cannibalize" (graphic, but a great word!) one another. Here is the essential relationship between the two series as I see it: **These two menus series stand on their own if you have students of fairly similar ability levels. This series, Differentiating Instruction With Menus for the Inclusive Classroom, provides menus for the lower level, on-level, and ELL students, whereas the original series provides menus for the on-level, advanced, and gifted students. If you work with a wide range of student abilities (from special needs to gifted), these two series can be used as companions. When used together, they provide a total of three tiered menu options for each topic of study.** The menus in this book are made to complement the menus in the original series, and they are coded so that they are easily distinguishable from one another. Each set of menus in this book is made up of a lower level menu, designated by a small triangle symbol in the upper right-hand corner, and a middle-level menu, designated by a small circle symbol in the upper right-hand corner. The menus contained in the corresponding volume of the original series (*Differentiating Instruction With Menus: Math* for grades 3–5) can be used as options for more advanced students.

Many teachers have told me how helpful the Differentiating Instruction With Menus books are and how they have modified the books to meet the needs of their students—by purchasing the K–2 books in addition to the 3–5 books for their fourth-grade classes, for instance, or by using menus from the 3–5 books in some of their ninth-grade classrooms. Teachers are always the first to tweak things to make them work, but I thought it would be great if those teachers had a tool that did all of that work for them. Thus, the Differentiating Instruction With Menus for the Inclusive Classroom series was born.

The menu designs used in this book (and the rest of the books in this series) reflect a successful modification technique that I started using in my classroom as the range of my students' ability levels widened. I experimented with many ways to use menus, from having all students use the same menu with the same expectations, to having everyone use the same menu with modified contracted expectations, to giving each student one of three leveled menus with some overlapping activities based on readiness, ability, and/or preassessment results. I found that if the ability levels among my students during a certain school year were closer, I could use one menu for everyone with only slight modifications; however, the greater the span of my students' abilities became, the more I needed a variety of leveled menus to reach everyone. Each book in the Differentiating Instruction With Menus for the Inclusive Classroom series, with its two leveled menus for the objectives covered, can fill this need, providing more options for students with diverse abilities in the inclusive classroom.

—Laurie E. Westphal

CHAPTER 1

Choice

Choice in the Inclusive Classroom

L et's begin by addressing the concept of the inclusive classroom. The term inclusive (vs. exclusive) leads one to believe that we are discussing a situation in which all students are included. In the simplest of terms, that is exactly what we are referring to as an inclusive classroom: a classroom that may have special needs students, on-level students, bilingual or ESL students, and gifted students. Although the concept is a simple one, the considerations are significant.

When thinking about the inclusive classroom and its unique ambiance, one must first consider the needs of the range of students within the classroom. Mercer and Lane (1996) stated it best in their assessment of the needs in an inclusive classroom:

> Students who are academically gifted, those who have had abundant experiences, and those who have demonstrated proficiency with lesson content typically tend to perform well when instruction is anchored at the "implicit" end of the instructional continuum. In contrast, low-performing students (i.e., students at risk for school failure, students with learning disabilities, and students with other special

 DOI: 10.4324/9781003234241-1

needs) and students with limited experience or proficiency with lesson content are most successful when instruction is explicit. Students with average academic performance tend to benefit most from the use of a variety of instructional methods that address individual needs. Instructional decisions for most students, therefore, should be based on assessment of individual needs. (pp. 230–231)

Acknowledging these varied and often contradictory needs that arise within an inclusive classroom can lead to frustration when trying to make one assignment or task fit everyone's needs. There are few—if any—traditional, teacher-directed lessons that can be implicit, explicit, and based on individual needs all at the same time. There is, however, one *technique* that tries to accomplish this: choice.

Choice: The Superman of Techniques?

Can the offering of appropriate choices really be the hero of the inclusive classroom? Can it leap buildings in a single bound and meet the needs of our implicit, explicit, and individual interests? Yes. By considering the use and benefits of choice, we can see that by offering choices, teachers really can meet the needs of the whole range of students in an inclusive classroom. Ask adults whether they would prefer to choose what to do or be told what to do, and of course, they will say they would prefer to have a choice. Students have the same feelings. Although they may not be experienced in making choices, they will make choices based on their needs, just as adults—which makes everyone involved in the inclusive experience a little less stressed and frustrated.

One benefit of choice is its ability to meet the needs of so many different students and their learning styles. The Dunedin College of Education (Keen, 2001) conducted a research study on the preferred learning styles of 250 gifted students. Students were asked to rank different learning options. Of the 13 different options described to the students, only one option did not receive at least one negative response: the option of having choice. All students have different learning styles and preferences, yet choice is the one option that meets all students' needs. Students, be they gifted or special needs, are going to choose what best fits their own learning styles and educational needs.

> ## "I am different in the way I do stuff. I like to build stuff with my hands."
>
> *—Sixth-grade student, when asked why he enjoyed activities that allow choice*

Another benefit of choice is a greater sense of independence for the students, some who have not had the opportunity to think about their own learning in the past. What a powerful feeling! Students will be designing and creating products based on what they envision, rather than what their teacher envisions. There is a possibility for more than one "right" product; all students can make products their own, no matter their level of ability. When students would enter my classroom, they had often been trained by previous teachers to produce exactly what the teacher wanted, not what the students thought would be best. Teaching my students that what they envisioned could be correct (and wonderful) was often a struggle. "Is this what you want?" and "Is this right?" were popular questions as we started the school year. Allowing students to have choices in the products they create to demonstrate their learning helps create independence at any age, within any ability level.

Strengthened student focus on the required content is a third benefit. When students have choices in the activities they wish to complete, they are more focused on the learning that leads to their choice product. Students become excited when they learn information that can help them develop a product they would like to create. Students pay close attention to instruction and have an immediate application for the knowledge being presented in class. Also, if students are focused, they are less likely to be off task during instruction.

The final benefit (although I am sure there are many more) is the simple fact that by offering varied choices at appropriate levels, you can address implicit instructional options, explicit instructional options, and individual needs without anyone getting overly frustrated or overworked. Many a great educator has referred to the idea that the best learning takes place when the students have a desire to learn and can feel successful while doing it. Some students have a desire to be taught information, others prefer to explore and learn things that are new to them; still others do not want to learn anything unless it is of interest to them. By choosing from different activities according to their interests and readiness, students stretch beyond what they already know, and by offering such choices, teachers create a void that needs to be filled. This void leads to a desire to learn.

A Point to Ponder: Making Good Choices Is a Skill

> "I wanted you to know, I never thought of [good choices as a skill] that way. That really opened my eyes."
>
> *—Kindergarten teacher, after hearing me discuss choice as a skill*

When we think of making a good choice as a skill, much like writing an effective paragraph, it becomes easy enough to understand the processes needed to encourage students to make their own choices. In keeping with this analogy, students could certainly figure out how to write on their own, and perhaps even how to compose sentences and paragraphs, by modeling other examples. Imagine, however, the progress and strength of the writing produced when students are given guidance and even the most basic of instruction on how to accomplish the task. The written piece is still their own, but the quality of the finished piece is much stronger when guidance is given during the process. The same is true with the quality of choices students can make in the classroom.

As with writing, students—especially those with special needs—could make choices on their own, but when the teacher provides background knowledge and assistance, the choices become more meaningful and the products richer. Although all students certainly need guidance, the on-level and special needs students often will need the most guidance; they have usually not been in an educational setting that has allowed them to experience different products, and the idea of choice can be new to them. Some students may have experienced only basic instructional choices, like choosing between two journal prompts or perhaps having the option of making either a poster or a PowerPoint presentation about the content being studied. Some may not have experienced even this level of choice. This lack of experience can cause frustration for both teacher and student.

Teaching Choices as a Skill

So, what is the best way to provide guidance and enable students to develop the skill of making good choices? First, choose the appropriate number of choices for your students. Although the goal might be to have students choose from nine different options, teachers might start by having their students choose from three predetermined choices the first day (if they were using a shape menu, for instance, students might choose a circle activity). Then, after those products had been created, students could choose from another three options a few days later, and perhaps from another three the following week. By breaking students' choices down, teachers reinforce how to approach or attack a more complex and/ or varied choice format in the future. All students can work up to making complex choices from longer lists of options as their choice skill level increases.

Second, students will need guidance on how to select the option that is right for them. They may not automatically gravitate towards options without an exciting and detailed description of each choice. For the most part, students have been trained to produce what the teacher requests, which means that when given a choice, they will usually choose what they think will please the teacher. This means that when the teacher discusses the different menu options, he or she has to be equally as excited about each option. The discussion of the different choices has to be animated and specific. For example, if the content is all very similar, the focus should be on the product: "If you want to do some singing, this one is for you!" or "If you want to write and draw, circle this one as a maybe!" Sometimes, options may differ based on both content and product, in which case both can be pointed out to students to assist them in making a good choice for themselves. "You have some different choices in our life cycle unit. If you want to do something with animals and drawing, check this one as a maybe. If you are thinking you want to do something with leaf collecting and making a speech, this one might be for you!" The more exposure students have to the processing the teacher provides, the more skillful they become in their choice making.

How Can Teachers Provide Choices?

> "I have seen my behavior issues significantly decrease when my students have choices. I wasn't expecting that at all—I thought that they would be off ask and harder to control."
>
> —*Fifth-grade inclusion teacher, when asked how his students with special needs respond to having choices*

When people go to a restaurant, the common goal is to find something on the menu to satisfy their hunger. Students come into our classrooms having a hunger, as well—a hunger for learning. Choice menus are a way of allowing our students to choose how they would like to satisfy that hunger. At the very least, a menu is a list of choices that students use to choose an activity (or activities) they would like to complete to show what they have learned. At best, it is a complex system in which students earn points by making choices from different areas of study. All menus should also incorporate a free-choice option for those "picky eaters" who would like to make a special order to satisfy their learning hunger.

The next few sections provide examples of the main types of menus that will be used in this book. Each menu has its own benefits, limitations or drawbacks, and time considerations. An explanation of the free-choice option and its management will follow the information on each type of menu.

Three Shape Menu

> "I like the flexibility of the Three Shape menu. I can give students just one strip of shapes or the entire menu depending on their readiness."
>
> —*Third-grade teacher*

Description

The Three Shape menu (see Figure 1.1) is a basic menu with a total of nine predetermined choices for students. The choices are created at

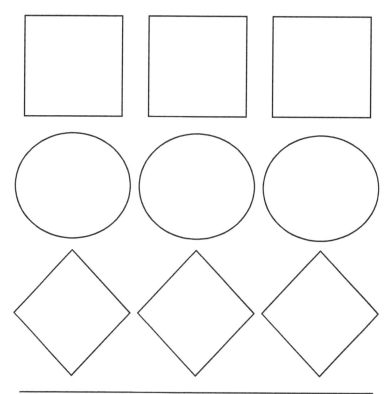

Figure 1.1. Three Shape menu.

the various levels of Bloom's Revised taxonomy (Anderson & Krathwohl, 2001) and incorporate different learning styles. All products carry the same weight for grading and have similar expectations for completion time and effort.

Benefits

Flexibility. This menu can cover one topic in depth, or three different objectives. When this menu covers just one objective, students have the option of completing three products: one from each shape group.

Friendly design. Students quickly understand how to use this menu. It is easy to explain how to make the choices based on the various shapes, and the shapes can be used to visually separate expectations (e.g., circles one week, squares the next).

Weighting. All products are equally weighted, so recording grades and maintaining paperwork is easily accomplished with this menu.

Short time period. They are intended for shorter periods of time, between 1–3 weeks.

Limitations

Few topics. These menus only cover one or three topics.

Time Considerations

These menus are usually intended for shorter amounts of completion time—at the most, they should take 3 weeks. If the menu focuses on one topic in depth, it could be completed in 1 week.

Tic-Tac-Toe Menu

> # "Sometimes I only liked two, but I had to do three."
>
> *—Second-grade student, when asked what he liked least about a menu used in his classroom*

Description

The Tic-Tac-Toe menu (see Figure 1.2) is a well-known, commonly used menu that contains a total of eight predetermined choices and, if appropriate, one free choice for students. Choices can be created at the same level of Bloom's Revised taxonomy or can be arranged in such a way to allow for the three different levels or content areas. If all choices have been created at the same level of Bloom's Revised taxonomy, then each choice carries the same weight for grading and has similar expectations for completion time and effort.

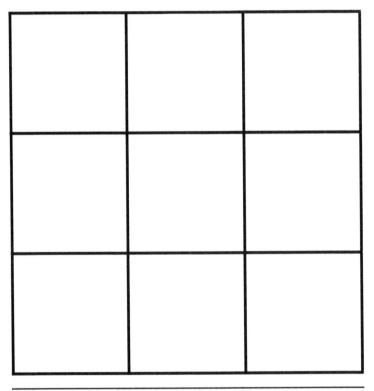

Figure 1.2. Tic-Tac-Toe menu.

Benefits

Flexibility. This menu can cover either one topic in depth or three different topics, objectives, or even content areas. When this menu covers just one objective and all tasks are from the same level of Bloom's Revised taxonomy, students have the option of completing three projects in a tic-tac-toe pattern, or simply picking three from the menu. When the menu covers three objectives or different levels of Bloom's Revised taxonomy, students will need to complete a tic-tac-toe pattern (either a vertical column or horizontal row) to be sure they have completed one activity from each objective or level.

Stretching. When students make choices on this menu, completing a row or column based on its design, they will usually face one choice that is out of their comfort zone, be it for its level of Bloom's Revised taxonomy, its product learning style, or its content. They will complete this "uncomfortable" choice because they want to do the other two in that row or column.

Friendly design. Students quickly understand how to use this menu. It is nonthreatening because it does not contain points, and therefore it seems to encourage students to stretch out of their comfort zones.

Weighting. All projects are equally weighted, so recording grades and maintaining paperwork is easily accomplished with this menu.

Short time period. These menus are intended for shorter periods of time, between 1–3 weeks.

Limitations

Few topics. These menus only cover one or three topics.

Student compromise. Although this menu does allow choice, a student will sometimes have to compromise and complete an activity he or she would not have chosen because it completes the required tic-tac-toe. (This is not always bad, though!)

Time Considerations

These menus are usually intended for shorter amounts of completion time—at the most, they should take 3 weeks with one product submitted each week. If the menu focuses on one topic in depth, it can be completed in 1 week.

List Menu

Description

The List menu (see Figure 1.3), or Challenge List, is a more complex menu than the Tic-Tac-Toe menu, with a total of at least 10 predetermined choices, each with its own point value, and at least one free choice for students. Choices are simply listed with assigned points based on the levels of Bloom's Revised taxonomy. The choices carry different weights and have different expectations for completion time and effort. A point criterion is set forth that equals 100%, and students choose how they wish to attain that point goal.

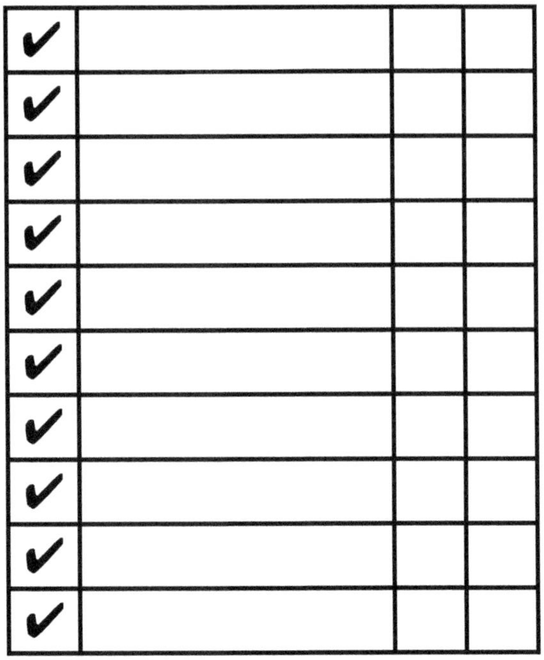

Benefits

Responsibility. Students have complete control over their grades. They really like the idea that they can guarantee their grades if they complete the required work. If they lose points on one of the chosen assignments, they can complete another to be sure they have met their goal points. This responsibility over their own grades also allows a shift in thinking about grades—whereas many students think of grades in terms of how the teacher judged their work, having control over their grades leads students to understand that they *earn* their grades.

Figure 1.3. List menu.

Different learning levels. This menu also has the flexibility to allow for individualized contracts for different learning levels within the classroom. Each student can contract for a certain number of points for his or her 100%.

Concept reinforcement. This menu allows for an in-depth study of material; however, with the different levels of Bloom's Revised taxonomy being represented, students who are still learning the concepts can choose some of the lower level point value projects to reinforce the basics before jumping into the higher level activities.

Variety. A list menu offers a larger variety of product choices. There is guaranteed to be a product of interest to everyone.

Limitations

One topic. This menu is best used for one topic in depth, so that students cannot miss any specific content.

Cannot guarantee objectives. If this menu is used for more than one topic, it is possible for a student not to have to complete an activity for each objective, depending on the choices he or she makes.

Preparation. Teachers need to have all materials ready at the beginning of the unit for students to be able to choose any of the activities on the list, which requires advanced planning. (Note: Once the materials are assembled, the menu is wonderfully low stress!)

Time Considerations

List menus are usually intended for shorter amounts of completion time—at the most, 2 weeks.

2-5-8 Menu

> ### "My favorite menu is the 2-5-8 kind. It's easy to understand, and I can pick just what I want to do."
> *—Fourth-grade student, when asked about his favorite type of menu*

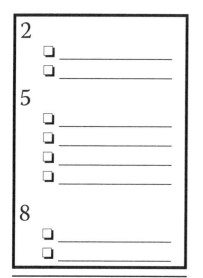

Figure 1.4. 2-5-8 menu.

Description

A 2-5-8 menu (see Figure 1.4; Magner, 2000) is a variation of a List menu, with a total of at least eight predetermined choices: two choices with a point value of two, at least four choices with a point value of five, and at least two choices with a point value of eight. Choices are assigned points based on the levels of Bloom's Revised taxonomy. Choices with a point value of two represent the "remember" and "understand" levels, choices with a point value of five represent the "apply" and "analyze" levels, and choices with a point value of eight represent the "evaluate" and "create" levels. All levels of choices carry different weights and have different expectations for completion time and effort. Students are expected to earn 10 points for a 100%. Students choose what combination they would like to use to attain that point goal.

Benefits

Responsibility. With this menu, students still have complete control over their grades.

Low stress. This menu is one of the shortest menus, and if students choose well, they could accomplish their goal by completing only two products. This menu is usually not as daunting as some of the longer, more complex menus.

Guaranteed activity. This menu's design is also set up in such a way that students must complete at least one activity at a higher level of Bloom's Revised taxonomy in order to reach their point goal.

Limitations

One topic. Although it can be used for more than one topic, this menu works best with an in-depth study of one topic.

No free choice. By nature, this menu does not allow students to propose their own free choice, because point values need to be assigned based on Bloom's Revised taxonomy.

Higher level thinking. Students may choose to complete only one activity at a higher level of thinking.

Time Considerations

The 2-5-8 menu is usually intended for a shorter amount of completion time—at the most, 1 week.

Baseball Menu

> ## "Wow. Wow, there's even more."
>
> *—Fifth-grade student, upon seeing her first baseball menu and then seeing even more options on the back*

Description

This menu (see Figure 1.5) is a baseball-based variation on the List menu with a total of at least 20 predetermined choices: choices are given values as singles, doubles, triples, or home runs based on the levels of Bloom's Revised taxonomy. Singles represent the remember and understand levels; doubles, the apply and analyze levels; triples, the evaluate level; and home runs, the create level. All levels of choices carry different weights and have different expectations for completion time and effort.

Figure 1.5. Baseball menu.

Students are expected to earn a certain number of runs (around all four bases) for a 100%. Students choose what combination they would like to use to attain that number of runs.

Benefits

Responsibility. With this menu, students still have complete control over their own grades.

Flexibility and variety. This menu allows for many choices at each level. Students should have no trouble finding something that catches their interest.

Theme. This menu has a fun theme that students enjoy and can be used throughout the classroom. A bulletin board can be set up with a baseball diamond, with each student having his or her own player who can move through the bases. Not only can students keep track of their own RBIs, but they can also have a visual reminder of what they have completed.

Limitations

One topic. This menu is best used for one all-encompassing unit with many objectives for in-depth study.

Preparation. With so many choices available to students, teachers should have all materials ready at the beginning of the unit for students to be able to choose any of the activities on the list. This sometimes is a consideration for space in the classroom.

One free choice. This menu also has only one opportunity for free choice for students.

Time Considerations

These menus are usually intended for a longer amount of completion time, depending on the number of runs required for a 100%. At most, these menus are intended for 4 or 5 weeks.

Free Choice in the Inclusive Classroom

"Free choice? What do you mean? I don't get it."
—*Fourth-grade student with special needs*

Most of the menus included in this book allow students to submit a free choice as a product. This free choice is a product of their choosing that addresses the content being studied and shows what the student has learned about the topic. Although this option is offered, students may not fully understand its benefits or immediately respond to the opportunity even after it has been explained. Although certain students have been offered choices before and may be very excited by the idea of taking charge of their own learning, our students with special needs may not have had much exposure to this concept. Their educational experiences tend to be objective-based and teacher-driven. This is not to say that they would not respond well to the idea of free choice; in fact, they can embrace it as enthusiastically as gifted students can. The most significant difference between these two groups successfully approaching free choice is the amount of content needed by the student before he or she embarks on a proposed option. Our students with special needs need to feel confident in their knowledge of the content and information before they are ready to step out on their own, propose their own ideas, and create their own products. Average students may be comfortable with less knowledge and structure.

With most of the menus, the students are allowed to submit a free choice for their teacher's consideration. Figure 1.6 shows two sample proposal forms that have been used many times successfully in my classroom. The form used is based on the type of menu being presented. If students are using the Tic-Tac-Toe or Three Shape menu, there is no need to submit a point proposal. A copy of these forms should be given to each student when each menu is first introduced. A discussion should be held with the students so they understand the expectations of a free choice. If students do not want to make a proposal using the proposal form after the teacher has discussed the entire menu and its activities, they can place the unused form in a designated place in the classroom. Others may want to use their form, and it is often surprising who wants to submit a proposal form after hearing about the opportunity!

Name: _____   Teacher's Approval: _____

Free-Choice Proposal Form for Point-Based Menu

Points Requested: _____   Points Approved: _____

<u>Proposal Outline</u>

1. What specific topic or idea will you learn about?

2. What criteria should be used to grade it? (Neatness, content, creativity, artistic value, etc.)

3. What will your product look like?

4. What materials will you need from the teacher to create this product?

Name: _____   Teacher's Approval: _____

Free-Choice Proposal Form

<u>Proposal Outline</u>

1. What specific topic or idea will you learn about?

2. What criteria should be used to grade it? (Neatness, content, creativity, artistic value, etc.)

3. What will your product look like?

4. What materials will you need from the teacher to create this product?

Figure 1.6. Sample proposal forms for free choice.

Proposal forms must be submitted before students begin working on their free-choice products. The teacher then knows what the students are working on, and the student knows the expectations the teacher has for that product. Once the project has been approved, the forms can easily be stapled to the student's menu sheet. The student can refer to the forms while developing the free-choice product, and when the grading takes place, the teacher can refer to the agreement for the graded features of the product.

Each part of the proposal form is important and needs to be discussed with students:

- *Name/Teacher's Approval.* The student must submit this form to the teacher for approval. The teacher will carefully review all of the information, discuss any suggestions or alterations with the student, if needed, and then sign the top.

- *Points Requested.* Found only on the point-based menu proposal form, this is where negotiation may need to take place. Students usually will submit their first request for a very high number (even the 100% goal). They tend to equate the amount of time something will take with the number of points it should earn. But please note that the points are always based on the levels of Bloom's Revised taxonomy. For example, a PowerPoint presentation with a vocabulary word quiz would get minimal points, although it may have taken a long time to create. If the students have not been exposed to the levels of Bloom's Revised taxonomy, this can be difficult to explain. You can always refer to the popular "Bloom's Verbs" to help explain the difference between time-consuming and higher level activities.

- *Points Approved.* Found only on the point-based menu proposal form, this is the final decision recorded by the teacher once the point haggling is finished.

- *Proposal Outline.* This is where the student will tell you everything about the product he or she intends to complete. These questions should be completed in such a way that you can really picture what the student is planning to complete. This also shows you that the student knows what he or she plans to complete.
  - *What specific topic or idea will you learn about?* Students need to be specific here. It is not acceptable to write "science" or "reading." This is where students look at the objectives of the project and choose which objective their project demonstrates.
  - *What criteria should be used to grade it?* Although there are rubrics for all of the projects that the students might create, it

is important for the students to explain what criteria are most important to evaluate the product. The student may indicate that the rubric being used for all of the predetermined projects is fine; however, he or she may also want to add other criteria here.

o *What will your product look like?* It is important that this response be as detailed as possible. If a student cannot express what it will look like, then he or she has probably not given the free-choice plan enough thought.

o *What materials will you need from the teacher to create this product?* This is an important consideration. Sometimes students do not have the means to purchase items for their project. This can be negotiated as well, but if you ask what students may need, they will often develop even grander ideas for their free choice.

CHAPTER 2

How to Use Menus in the Inclusive Classroom

There are different ways to use instructional menus in the inclusive classroom. In order to decide how to implement each menu, the following questions should be considered: How much prior knowledge of the topic being taught do the students have before the unit or lesson begins, how confident are your students in making choices and working independently, and how much intellectually appropriate information is readily available for students to obtain on their own?

There are many ways to use menus in the classroom. One way that is often overlooked is using menus to review or build background knowledge before a unit begins. This is frequently used when students have had exposure to upcoming content in the past, perhaps during the previous year's instruction or through similar life experiences. Although they may have been exposed to the content previously, students may not remember the details of the content at the level needed to proceed with the upcoming unit immediately. A shorter menu covering the previous years' objectives can be provided in the weeks prior to the new unit so that students have the opportunity to recall and engage with the information in a meaningful way. They are then ready to take it to a deeper level during the unit. For example, 2 weeks before starting a unit on graphs, the teacher may select a short menu on reading graphs, knowing that

DOI: 10.4324/9781003234241-2

the students have covered the content in the past and should be able to successfully work independently on the menu by engaging their prior knowledge. Students work on products from the menu as anchor activities and homework throughout the 2 weeks preceding the graphing unit, with all products being submitted prior to the unit's initiation. This way, the students have been in the "graphing frame of mind" independently for 2 weeks and are ready to investigate the topic further.

Introducing menus for enrichment and supplementary activities is the most common way of using menus. In this case, the students usually do not have a lot of background knowledge, and information about the topic may not be readily available to all students. The teacher will introduce the menu and the activities at the beginning of a unit. The teacher will then progress through the content at the normal rate, using his or her own curricular materials and periodically allowing class time and homework time throughout the unit for students to work on their menu choices to promote a deeper understanding of the lessons being taught. This method is very effective, as it incorporates an immediate use for the content the teacher is covering. For example, at the beginning of a unit on fractions, the teacher may introduce the menu with the explanation that students may not yet have all of the knowledge needed to complete all of their choices. The teacher would explain that during the unit, more content would be provided and students would be prepared to work on new choices. If students wanted to work ahead, they could certainly find the information on their own, but that would not be required. Although gifted students often see this as a challenge and begin to investigate concepts mentioned in the menu before the teacher has discussed them, other students begin to develop questions about the concepts and are ready to ask them when the teacher covers the material. This helps build an immense pool of background knowledge and possible content questions before the topic is even discussed in the classroom. As teachers, we constantly fight the battle of trying to get students to read ahead or come to class already prepared for discussion. By introducing a menu at the beginning of a unit and allowing students to complete products as instruction progresses, we encourage the students to naturally investigate the information and come to class prepared without having to make preparation a separate requirement.

Another option for using menus in the classroom is to replace certain curricular activities the teacher uses to teach the specified content. In this case, the students may have some limited background knowledge about the content and have information readily available for them among their classroom resources. This situation allows the teacher to pick and choose which aspects of the content need to be directly taught to the students in large or small groups and which can be appropriately learned and reinforced through product menus. The unit is then designed using formal instructional large-group lessons, smaller informal group lessons, and specific menu days during which the students use the menu to reinforce the prior knowledge they have already gained. In order for this option to be effective, the teacher must feel very comfortable with the students' prior knowledge level and their readiness to work independently. Another variation on this method is using the menus to drive center or station activities. Centers have many different functions in the classroom—most importantly, reinforcing the instruction that has already taken place. Rather than having a set rotation for centers, the teacher may use the menu activities as enrichment or as supplementary activities during center time for those students who need more than just reinforcement; centers can be set up with the materials students would need to complete various products.

Yet another option for menu use is the use of mini-lessons, with the menus driving the accompanying classroom activities. This method is best used when the majority of the students have similar amounts of knowledge about the topic. The teacher can design 15–20-minute mini-lessons in which students quickly review basic concepts that are already familiar to them and are then exposed to the new content in a short and concise way. Then students are turned loose to choose an activity on the menu to show that they understand the concept. It is important that the students either have some prior knowledge on the content or be effective at working independently, because the lesson cycle is shorter in this use of menus. Using menus in this way does shorten the amount of time teachers have to use the guided practice step of the lesson, so all instruction and examples should be carefully selected. By using the menus in this way, the teacher avoids the one-size-fits-all independent practice portion of the lesson. If there are still a few students struggling, they can be pulled into a small-group situation while the other students work on their choices from the menu. Another important consideration is the independence level of the students. In order for this use of menus to be effective, students will need to be able to work independently for up to 20 minutes after the mini-lesson. Because students are often interested in the product they have chosen, this is not a critical issue, but it is still one worth mentioning as teachers consider how they would like to use various menus in their classroom.

Introducing and Using Leveled Menus With Students

The menus in this book are tiered versions of the menus found in its companion series, Differentiation Instruction With Menus. Although the topics and objectives are alike, these menus may have different values assigned to the same tasks, slightly different wording for similar tasks, the same product options in a menu of a different format, or even tasks that are only available on certain menus. All of these minor modifications make certain menus more appropriate for different students based on their readiness, interests, and ability levels.

As we all know, students tend to compare answers, work, and ideas, and the same goes for their menu choices. Although students may notice the slight aforementioned differences, it may not be an issue when students are working in ability groups, as students are comfortable with not having the exact same options as their classmates. It may also not be an issue when the menus are presented in a matter-of-fact manner, as everyone is getting a menu that was especially chosen for him or her, so students may notice some differences between their menus. Students should rest assured that target numbers (e.g., a goal of 100 points must be met to receive a 100%) is equal for all of the menus provided, and that the activities most often preferred by students are found on all of the menus. Students should also know that most of the menus have a free-choice proposal option, so if they really want to do one of the activities found on another menu in the classroom, they are welcome to submit a free-choice proposal form in order to complete that activity. By presenting tiered menus with confidence and by making it clear that each menu is selected specifically for each student, you can make students much more willing to accept the system and proceed within the confines that you have set.

That being said, you may still have a few students who say, in that dreaded nasal, accusatory tone, "That's still not fair!" When I first starting using leveled menus, I heard a few comments like this. They quickly dissipated with my standard and practiced responses. Of course, the first response (which they do not always appreciate) is that fair is not the same as equal. I know students do not like to hear this response, as it is patently true and therefore difficult to dispute. Secondly, I remind students that everyone has different strengths, and the menus are distributed in order to emphasize students' strengths. Again, they know this; they just do not like to acknowledge it. Lastly, if the students are being especially surly, I sometimes have to play the "parent card," meaning that I am the teacher and so have the right to do what I feel is best for each student. This last option is nonnegotiable, and although students may not like it, they understand the tone and sentiment, as they have usually experienced it at home.

The bottom line when it comes to tiered menu use is that students will respond to the use of different menus within one classroom based on how the teacher presents or reacts to it. In the past, when I have used different formats, I have addressed the format or obvious differences in a matter-of-fact manner, by saying things such as, "I have spiced things up with this menu and have three different ones that I will pass out. You may receive one that is different than your neighbor's, but whichever one you receive is going to be lots of fun for you!" Other times, when the menus are very similar in their formats and graphics, I simply distribute them and address concerns when they are brought up. For the most part, students are more likely to simply go with what they have been given when the differences in menus are presented confidently, without being open to debate or complaint.

CHAPTER 3

Guidelines for Products

This chapter outlines the different types of products included in the featured menus, as well as the guidelines and expectations for each. It is very important that students know exactly what the expectations of a completed product are when they choose to work on it. By discussing these expectations before students begin and having the information readily available ahead of time, you will limit the frustration on everyone's part.

$1 Contract

Consideration should be given to the cost of creating the products featured on any menu. The resources available to students vary within a classroom, and students should not be graded on the amount of materials they can purchase to make a product look better. These menus are designed to equalize the resources students have available. The materi-

DOI: 10.4324/9781003234241-3

als for most products are available for less than a dollar and can often be found in a teacher's classroom as part of the classroom supplies. If a product requires materials from the student, there is a $1 contract as part of the product criteria. This is a very important piece in the explanation of the product. First of all, by limiting the amount of money a child can spend, teachers create an equal amount of resources for all students. Second, this practice actually encourages a more creative product. When students are limited by the amount of materials they can readily purchase, they often have to use materials from home in new and unique ways. Figure 3.1 is a sample of the contract that has been used many times in my classroom with various products.

$1 Contract

I did not spend more than $1.00 on my _____.

_____   _____
Student Signature   Date

My child, _____, did not spend more than $1.00 on the product he or she created.

_____   _____
Parent Signature   Date

Figure 3.1. $1 contract.

The Products

Table 3.1 contains a list of the products used in this book. These products were chosen for their flexibility in meeting different learning styles, as well as for being products many teachers are already using in their classroom. They have been arranged by learning style—visual, kinesthetic, or auditory—and each menu has been designed to include products from all of these learning styles. Of course, some of the products may represent more than one style of learning, depending on how

Table 3.1
Products

Visual	Kinesthetic	Auditory
Acrostic	Collection	Interview
Advertisement	Commercial	News Report
Book Cover	Concentration Cards	Play
Brochure/Pamphlet	Diorama	PowerPoint—Speaker
Bumper Sticker	Flipbook	Song/Rap
Cartoon/Comic Strip	Game	Speech
Children's Book	Mobile	Student-Taught
Collage	Model	Lesson
Commercial	Play	Video
Crossword Puzzle	Product Cube	You Be the Person
Diary	Puppet/Puppet Show	Presentation
Dictionary	Science Experiment	
Drawing	Trophy	
Greeting Card	Video	
Instruction Card		
Letter		
List		
Map		
Mind Map		
Newspaper Article		
Poster		
PowerPoint—Stand-Alone		
Questionnaire		
Recipe/Recipe Card		
Report		
Scrapbook		
Sculpture		
Story		
Summary		
Three Facts and a Fib		
Timeline		
Trading Cards		
Venn Diagram		
Windowpane		
Worksheet		

they are presented or implemented. Some of these products are featured in the menus more often than others, but students may choose the less common products as free-choice options.

Product Frustrations

One of the biggest frustrations that accompany the use of these various products on menus is the barrage of questions about the products themselves. Students can become so wrapped up in the products and the criteria for creating them that they do not focus on the content being presented. This is especially true when menus are introduced to the class. Students can spend an exorbitant amount of time asking the teacher about the products mentioned on the menu. When this happens, what should have been a 10–15-minute menu introduction turns into 45–50 minutes of discussion about product expectations. In order to facilitate the introduction of the menu products, teachers may consider showing students examples of the product(s) from the previous year. Although this can be helpful, it can also lead to additional frustration on the part of both the teacher and the students. Some students may not feel that they can produce a product as nice, as big, as special, or as (you fill in the blank) as the example, or when shown an example, students might interpret that as meaning that the teacher would like something exactly like the one he or she showed to students. To avoid this situation, I would propose that when using examples, the example students are shown be a "blank" one that demonstrates how to create only the shell of the product. If an example of a windowpane is needed, for instance, students might be shown a blank piece of paper that is divided into six panes. The students can then take the "skeleton" of the product and make it their own as they create their own version of the windowpane using their information.

Product Guidelines

Most frustrations associated with products can be addressed proactively through the use of standardized, predetermined product guidelines, to be shared with students prior to them creating any products. These product guidelines are designed in a specific yet generic way, such that any time throughout the school year that the students select a product, that product's guidelines will apply. A beneficial side effect of using set guidelines for a product is the security it creates. Students are often reticent to try something new, as doing so requires taking a risk.

Traditionally, when students select a product, they ask questions about creating it, hope they remember and understood all of the details, and turn it in. It can be quite a surprise when they receive the product back and realize that it was not complete or was not what was expected. As you can imagine, students may not want to take the risk on something new the next time; they often prefer to do what they know and be successful. Through the use of product guidelines, students can begin to feel secure in their choice before they start working on a new product. If they are not feeling secure, they tend to stay within their comfort zone.

The product guidelines for menu products included in this book, as well as some potential free-choice options, are included in an easy-to-read card format (see Figure 3.2) with graphics that depict the guidelines and help the students remember the important criteria for each product. (The guidelines for some products, such as summaries, are omitted because teachers often have different criteria for these products.) Once the products and/or menus have been selected, there are many options available to share this information.

There really is no one "right way" to share the product guideline information with your students. It all depends on their abilities and needs. Some teachers choose to duplicate and distribute all of the product guidelines pages to students at the beginning of the year so that each child has his or her own copy while working on products. As another option, a few classroom sets can be created by gluing each product guideline card onto a separate index card, hole punching the corner of each card, and placing all of the cards on a metal ring. These ring sets can be placed in a central location or at centers where students can borrow and return them as they work on their products. This allows for the addition of products as they are introduced. Some teachers prefer to introduce product guidelines as students experience products on their menus. In this case, product guidelines from the menu currently assigned can be enlarged, laminated, and posted on a bulletin board for easy access during classroom work. Some teachers may choose to reproduce each menu's specific product guidelines on the back of the menu. No matter which method teachers choose to share the information with the students, they will save themselves a lot of time and frustration by having the product guidelines available for student reference (e.g., "Look at your product guidelines—I think that will answer your question").

Acrostic

- At least 8.5" x 11"
- Neatly written or typed
- Target word will be written down the left side of the paper
- Each descriptive word chosen must begin with one of the letters from the target word
- Each descriptive word chosen must be related to the target word

Advertisement

- At least 8.5" x 11"
- Should include a slogan
- Color picture of item or service
- Include price, if appropriate

Book Cover

- Front Cover—title, author, image
- Cover Inside Flap—summary of book
- Back Inside Flap—brief biography of author
- Back Cover—comments about book
- Spine—title and author
- May be placed on actual book, but does not have to be

Brochure/Pamphlet

- At least 8.5" x 11"
- Must be in three-fold format; front fold has title and picture
- Must have both pictures and information
- Information should be in paragraph form with at least five facts included

Figure 3.2. Product guidelines.

Bumper Sticker

- Uses a regular piece of paper cut in half lengthwise
- Must have a picture to meet the task
- Must have a motto

Cartoon/Comic Strip

- At least 8.5" x 11"
- At least six cells
- Must have meaningful dialogue
- Must have color

Children's Book

- Must have cover with book's title and author's name
- Must have at least five pages
- Each page should have an illustration to accompany the story
- Should be neatly written or typed
- Can be developed on the computer

Collage

- At least 8.5" x 11"
- Pictures must be neatly cut from magazines or newspapers (no clip art)
- Label items as required in task

Figure 3.2. Continued.

Commercial

- Must be between 2–3 minutes
- Script must be turned in before commercial is presented
- Can be presented live to an audience or recorded
- Should have props or some form of costume
- Can include more than one person

Concentration Cards

- At least 20 index cards (10 matching sets)
- Can use both pictures and words
- Information should be placed on just one side of each card
- Include an answer key that shows the matches
- All cards must be submitted in a carrying bag

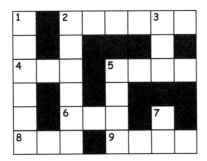

Crossword Puzzle

- Must include at least 20 significant words or phrases
- Clues must be appropriate
- Include puzzle and answer key

Diary

- Neatly written or typed
- Include appropriate number of entries
- Include date, if appropriate
- Must be written in first person

Figure 3.2. Continued.

Dictionary

- Neatly written or made on the computer
- Definition should be in student's own words
- Has a clear picture for each word
- Pictures can be drawn or from the computer

Diorama

- At least 4" x 5" x 8"
- Must be self-standing
- All interior space covered with relevant pictures and information
- Name written on back in permanent ink
- $1 contract signed
- Informational/title card attached to diorama

Drawing

- Must be at least 8.5" x 11"
- Must include color
- Must be neatly drawn by hand
- Must have title
- Name should be written on the back

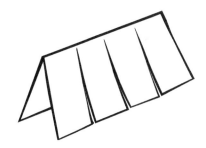

Flipbook

- At least 8.5" x 11" folded in half
- All information or opinions must be supported by facts
- Created with the correct number of flaps cut into top
- Color is optional
- Name written on the back

Figure 3.2. Continued.

Game

- At least four thematic game pieces
- At least 25 colored/thematic squares
- At least 20 question/activity cards
- A thematic title on the board
- A complete set of rules for playing the game
- At least the size of an open file folder

Greeting Card

- Front–colored pictures, words optional
- Front Inside–personal note related to topic
- Back Inside–greeting or saying, must meet product criteria
- Back Outside–logo, publisher, and price for card

Instruction Card

- Created on heavy paper or card
- Neatly written or typed
- Uses color drawings
- Provides instructions stated

Interview

- Must have at least five questions important to topic being studied
- Questions and answers must be neatly written or typed
- Must include name of person being interviewed
- Must get teacher or parent permission before interviewing person

Figure 3.2. Continued.

Letter

- Neatly written or typed
- Must use proper letter format
- At least three paragraphs
- Must follow type of letter stated in menu (friendly, persuasive, informational)

List

- Neatly written or made on the computer
- Has the number of items required
- Is as complete as possible
- Alphabet lists need words or phrases for each letter of the alphabet except X

Map

- At least 8.5" x 11"
- Accurate information
- Must include at least 10 relevant locations
- Includes compass rose, legend, scale, key

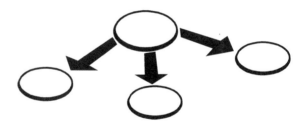

Mind Map

- At least 8.5" x 11" unlined paper
- Must have one central idea
- Follow the "no more than four rule" (there should be no more than four words coming from any one word)

Figure 3.2. Continued.

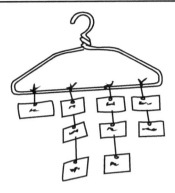

Mobile

- At least 10 pieces of related information
- Includes color and pictures
- At least three layers of hanging information
- Be able to hang in a balanced way

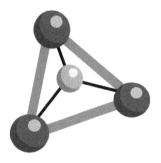

Model

- At least 8" x 8" x 12"
- Parts of model must be labeled
- Should be to scale when appropriate
- Must include a title card
- Name permanently written on model

News Report

- Must address the who, what, where, when, why, and how of topic
- Script of report turned in with project (or before if performance will be live)
- Can be either live or recorded

Newspaper Article

- Must be informational in nature
- Must follow standard newspaper format
- Must include picture with caption that supports article
- At least three paragraphs
- Neatly written or typed

Figure 3.2. Continued.

Play

- Must be between 3–5 minutes
- Script must be turned in before play is presented
- Must be presented to an audience
- Should have props or some form of costume
- Can include more than one person

Poster

- Should be size of standard poster board
- At least five pieces of important information
- Must have title
- Must have both words and pictures
- Name must be written on back

PowerPoint – Speaker

- At least 10 informational slides and one title slide with student's name
- No more than two words per page
- Slides must have color and at least one graphic per page
- Animations are optional but should not distract from information being presented
- Presentation should be timed and flow with speech being given

PowerPoint – Stand-Alone

- At least 10 informational slides and one title slide with student's name
- No more than 10 words per page
- Slides must have color and at least one graphic per page
- Animations are optional but must not distract from information being presented

Figure 3.2. Continued.

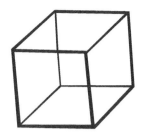

Product Cube

- All six sides of cube must be filled with information
- Name must be printed neatly on bottom of one side of cube

Puppet

- Puppet must be handmade and must have a moveable mouth
- A list of supplies used to make puppet must be turned in with puppet
- $1 contract signed
- If used in puppet show, all puppet show criteria must also be met

Puppet Show

- Must be between 3–5 minutes
- Script must be turned in before show is presented
- Must be presented to an audience
- Should have a different puppet for each role

Questionnaire

- Neatly written or typed
- At least 10 questions with possible answers
- At least one answer that requires a written response
- Questions must be related to topic being studied

Figure 3.2. Continued.

Recipe/Recipe Card

- Must be written neatly or typed on a piece of paper or index card
- Must have list of ingredients with measurements for each
- Must have numbered steps that explain how to make the recipe

Report

- Neatly written or made on the computer
- Must have enough information to address topic
- Information has to be student's own words, not copied from a book or the Internet

Scrapbook

- Cover of scrapbook must have meaningful title and student's name
- Must have at least five themed pages
- Each page must have at least one picture
- All photos must have captions

Sculpture

- Cannot be larger than 2 feet tall
- Must include any specified items
- Name should be written on bottom
- Must not use any valuable materials

Figure 3.2. Continued.

Song/Rap

- Words must make sense
- Can be presented to an audience or recorded
- Written words will be turned in
- Should be at least 1 minute in length

Speech

- Must be at least 2 minutes in length
- Should not be read from written paper
- Note cards can be used
- Written speech must be turned in
- Voice must be clear, loud, and easy to understand

Story

- Must be neatly written or typed
- Must have all elements of a well-written story (setting, characters, problem, events, resolution)
- Must be appropriate length to allow for story elements

Three Facts and a Fib

- Can be written, typed, or created using Microsoft PowerPoint
- Must include exactly four statements: three true statements and one false statement
- False statement should not obvious
- Brief paragraph should be included that explains why the fib is false

Figure 3.2. Continued.

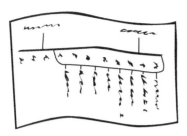

Timeline

- No bigger than standard-sized poster board
- Must be divided into equal intervals of time
- Must contain at least 10 important dates
- Must have an explanation of at least two sentences for each date about its importance

Trading Cards

- Include at least 10 cards
- Each card should be at least 3" x 5"
- Each should have a colored picture
- At least three facts on the subject of the card
- Cards must have information on both sides
- All cards must be submitted in a carrying bag

Trophy

- Must be at least 6 inches tall
- Must have a base with the winner's name and the name of the award written neatly or typed on it
- Top of trophy must be appropriate to the award
- Name should be written on the bottom of the award
- Must be an originally designed trophy (avoid reusing a trophy from home)

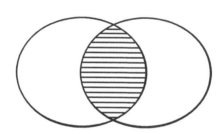

Venn Diagram

- At least 8.5" x 11"
- Shapes should be thematic and neatly drawn
- Must have a title for entire diagram and a title for each section
- Must have at least six items in each section of diagram
- Name must be written on back

Figure 3.2. Continued.

Video

- Must be recorded
- Must turn in written plan or storyboard with project
- Student must arrange to use own video recorder or allow teacher at least 3 days' notice for use of recorder
- Must cover important information about the project
- Name must be written on video or disc

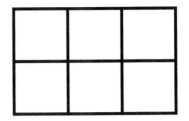

Windowpane

- At least 8.5" x 11" unlined paper
- At least six squares
- Each square must include a picture and words
- Name should be recorded on bottom right-hand corner of front

Worksheet

- Must be 8.5" x 11"
- Neatly written or typed
- Must cover specific topic or question in detail
- Must be creative in design
- Must have at least one graphic
- Must turn in corresponding answer key

You Be the Person Presentation

- Take on the role of the person
- Cover at least five important facts about the life of the person
- Should be between 2–4 minutes in length
- Script must be turned in before information is presented
- Should present to an audience and answer questions while staying in character
- Must have props or some form of costume

Figure 3.2. Continued.

CHAPTER 4

Rubrics

> "All the grading of the projects kept me from using menus before. The rubric makes it easier, though, and [the different projects] are fun to see."
>
> —*Fourth-grade teacher, when asked to explain reservations about using menus*

The most common reason teachers feel uncomfortable with menus is the need for equal grading. Teachers often feel that it is easier to grade the same type of product made by all of the students than to grade a large number of different products, none of which looks like any other. The great equalizer for hundreds of different products is a generic rubric that can cover all of the important qualities of an excellent product.

 DOI: 10.4324/9781003234241-4

All-Purpose Rubric

Figure 4.1 is an example of a rubric that has been classroom tested with various menus. This rubric can be used with any point value activity presented in a menu, as there are five criteria and the columns represent full points, half points, and no points.

There are different ways that this rubric can be shared with students. Some teachers prefer to provide it when a menu is presented to students. The rubric can be reproduced on the back of the menu along with its guidelines. The rubric can also be given to students to keep in their folders with their product guideline cards so they always know the expectations as they complete projects throughout the school year. Some teachers prefer to keep a master copy for themselves and post an enlarged copy of the rubric on a bulletin board, or provide one copy for parents during open house so that they understand how their children's menu products will be graded.

No matter how the rubric is shared with students, the first time they see this rubric, it should be explained to them in detail, especially the last column, titled "Self." It is very important that students self-evaluate their projects. This column can provide a unique perspective on the project as it is being graded. Note: This rubric was designed to be specific enough that students will understand the criteria the teacher is seeking, but general enough that they can still be as creative as they like while making their products.

Student Presentation Rubric

Although the all-purpose rubric can be used for all activities, there is one occasion in math that seems to warrant a special rubric: student presentations. A student presentation can be a unique situation with many details that should be considered separately.

Student presentations can be difficult to evaluate, especially when done for a class that students do not feel is related to language. You may get the question, "Why do we have to write and present if this is a math class?" With these types of presentations, objectivity must be the first consideration. The objectivity can be addressed through a very specific presentation rubric that states what is expected of the speaker. The rubric will need to be discussed and various criteria demonstrated before the students begin preparing presentations. The second consideration is that of the audience and its interest. How frustrating it can be to grade 30

Name: _____

All-Purpose Product Rubric

	Excellent (Full Points)	Good (Half Points)	Poor (No Points)	Self
Completeness Is everything included in the product?	All information needed is included. Meets product guidelines.	Some important information is missing. Meets product guidelines.	Most important information is missing or does not meet guidelines.	
Creativity Is the product original?	Information is creative. Graphics are original. Presentations are unique.	Information is creative. Graphics are not original or were found on the computer.	There is no evidence of new thoughts or perspectives in the product.	
Correctness Is all the information included correct?	All information in the product is correct.		Any portion of the information included is incorrect.	
Appropriate Communication Is the information well communicated?	All information is neat, easy to read, or—if presented—easy to understand.	Most of the product is neat, easy to read, and—if presented easy to understand.	The product is not neat or is not easy to read.	
Effort and Time Did student put significant effort into the product?	Effort is obvious.		The product does not show significant effort.	

Figure 4.1. All-purpose product rubric.

presentations when the audience is not paying attention! This issue can be solved by allowing your audience to be directly involved in the presentation. Once all of the students have been familiarized with the student presentation rubric (see Figure 4.2), when they receive their own rubrics with which to give feedback to their classmates (see Figure 4.3), they are quite comfortable with the criteria. Students are asked to rank their classmates on a scale of 1–10 in the areas of content, flow, and the prop chosen to enhance the presentation. They are also asked to state two things the presenter did well. Although most students understand that this should be a positive experience for the presenter, you may want to review guidelines for what students should *not* include in their feedback. For example, if the presenter dropped his or her product and had to pick it up, then the presenter already knows this; it does not need to be noted again. The feedback should be positive and specific. Rather than writing, "Great job," a student should write something specific, such as, "I could hear you speak loudly and clearly throughout the entire presentation," or, "You had great graphics!" These types of comments really make the students take note of areas where they could improve and feel great about their presentations. The teacher should not be surprised to note that the students often look through all of their classmates' feedback and comments before ever consulting the rubric completed by the teacher. Once students have completed feedback forms for a presenter, the forms can then be gathered at the end of each presentation, stapled together, and given to the presenter at the end of the class.

Name: _____

Student Presentation Rubric

	Excellent	Good	Fair	Poor	Self
Content Complete Did the presentation include everything it should?	30 Presentation included all important information about topic being presented.	20 Presentation covered most of the important information, but one key idea was missing.	10 Presentation covered some of the important information, but more than one key idea was missing.	0 Presentation covered information, but the information was trivial or fluff.	
Content Correct Was the information presented accurate?	30 All information presented was accurate.	20 All information presented was correct, with a few unintentional errors that were quickly corrected.	Not applicable: There is no middle ground when it comes to correctness of content.	0 Any information presented was not correct.	
Prop Did the speaker have at least one prop that was directly related to the presentation?	20 Presenter had a prop and it complemented the presentation.	12 Presenter had a prop, but it was not the best choice.	4 Presenter had a prop, but there was no clear reason for it.	0 Presenter had no prop.	
Content Consistent Did the speaker stay on topic?	10 Presenter stayed on topic 100% of the time.	7 Presenter stayed on topic 90–99% of the time.	4 Presenter stayed on topic 80–89% of the time.	0 It was hard to tell what the topic was.	
Flow Was the speaker familiar and comfortable with the material so that it flowed well?	10 Presentation flowed well. Speaker did not stumble over words.	7 Presenter had some flow problems, but they did not distract from information.	4 Some flow problems interrupted the presentation, and presenter seemed flustered.	0 Constant flow problems occurred, and information was not presented so that it could be understood.	
				Total Grade:	

Figure 4.2. Student presentation rubric.

Topic: _____ **Student's Name:** _____

On a scale of 1–10, rate the following areas:

Content (How in depth was the information? How well did the speaker know the information? Was the information correct? Could the speaker answer questions?)		Give one short reason why you gave this number.
Flow (Did the presentation flow smoothly? Did the speaker appear confident and ready to speak?)		Give one short reason why you gave this number.
Prop (Did the speaker explain his or her prop? Did this choice seem logical? Was it the best choice?)		Give one short reason why you gave this number.

Comments: Below, write two things that you think the presenter did well:

1. _____

_____

2. _____

_____

- -

Topic: _____ **Student's Name:** _____

On a scale of 1–10, rate the following areas:

Content (How in depth was the information? How well did the speaker know the information? Was the information correct? Could the speaker answer questions?)		Give one short reason why you gave this number.
Flow (Did the presentation flow smoothly? Did the speaker appear confident and ready to speak?)		Give one short reason why you gave this number.
Prop (Did the speaker explain his or her prop? Did this choice seem logical? Was it the best choice?)		Give one short reason why you gave this number.

Comments: Below, write two things that you think the presenter did well:

1. _____

_____

2. _____

_____

Figure 4.3. Student feedback form.

The Menus

How to Use the Menu Pages

Each menu in this section has:
- an introduction page for the teacher;
- a lower level content menu, indicated by a triangle (▲) in the upper right-hand corner;
- a middle-level content menu, indicated by a circle (●) in the upper right-hand corner;
- any specific guidelines for the menu; and
- activities mentioned in the menu.

Introduction Pages

The introduction pages are meant to provide an overview of each menu. They are divided into five areas:

1. *Objectives Covered Through These Menus and These Activities.* This area will list all of the objectives that the menus can address. Menus are arranged in such a way that if students complete the guidelines set forth in the instructions for the menus, all of these objectives will be covered.

2. *Materials Needed by Students for Completion.* For each menu, it is expected that the teacher will provide, or students will have access to, the following materials:
   - lined paper;
   - glue;
   - crayons, colored pencils, or markers; and
   - blank 8.5" x 11" white paper.

   The introduction page also includes a list of additional materials that may be needed by students as they complete either menu. Any materials listed that are used in only one of the two menus are designated with the menu's corresponding code (either triangle or circle). Students do have the choice about the menu items they can complete, so it is possible that the teacher will not need all of these materials for every student.

3. *Special Notes on the Use of These Menus.* Some menus allow students to choose to present demonstrations, experiments, songs, or PowerPoint presentations to their classmates. This section will give any special tips on managing these student presentations. This section will also share any tips to consider for a specific activity.

4. *Time Frame.* Most menus are best used in at least a 1-week time frame. Some are better suited to more than 2 weeks. This section will give an overview about the best time frame for completing the entire menu, as well as options for shorter time periods. If teachers do not have time to devote to an entire menu, they can certainly choose the 1–2-day option for any menu topic students are currently studying.

5. *Suggested Forms.* This is a list of the rubrics, templates, and reproducibles that should be available for students as the menus are introduced. If a menu has a free-choice option, the appropriate proposal form also will be listed here.

CHAPTER 5

Whole Numbers and Operations

 DOI: 10.4324/9781003234241-5

Place Value

List Menus

Objectives Covered Through These Menus and These Activities
- Students will find the place value of integers in a five-digit number.
- Students will gain an understanding of larger numbers.
- Students will locate and analyze how larger numbers are used in our everyday world.

Materials Needed by Students for Completion
- *How Much Is a Million?* by David M. Schwartz
- Poster board or large white paper
- Microsoft PowerPoint or other slideshow software
- Newspapers
- World map
- Graph paper or Internet access (for crossword puzzles)
- Rulers
- Newspapers
- Coat hangers (for mobiles)
- Index cards (for mobiles)
- String (for mobiles)
- Blank index cards (for concentration cards and trading cards)
- Materials for scrapbooks

Time Frame
- 1–2 weeks—Students are given the menus as the unit is started, and the guidelines and point expectations are discussed. Because these menus cover one topic in depth, the teacher will go over all of the options on the menus and have students place check marks in the boxes next to the activities they are most interested in completing. As instruction continues, the activities are completed by students and submitted for grading.
- 1–2 days—The teacher chooses an activity from an objective to use with the entire class during that lesson time.

Suggested Forms
- All-purpose rubric
- Point-based free-choice proposal form

Place Value: Side 1

Guidelines:

1. You may complete as many of the activities listed within the time period.
2. You may choose any combination of activities.
3. Your goal is 100 points. You may earn up to _____ points extra credit.
4. You may be as creative as you like within the guidelines listed below.
5. You must show your plan to your teacher by _____.
6. Activities may be turned in at any time during the working time period. They will be graded and recorded on this sheet as you continue to work, so keep it safe!

Plan to Do	Activity to Complete (Side 1: 15–25 points)	Point Value	Date Completed	Points Earned
	Create a flipbook to show the different place values a number can have. Place an example under each flap.	15		
	Create a set of concentration cards with numbers and their place values to help your classmates practice.	15		
	Find the populations of five cities in your state. Put them in order from least to greatest.	15		
	Create a mobile to represent the population of your state. For each number, give its place value.	15		
	Complete a classmate's crossword puzzle.	15		
	Design a folded quiz book about the place values we are studying.	20		
	Create a number crossword puzzle to help your classmates practice place value.	25		
	Create a set of trading cards, one for each place value. Be creative in the facts you record about each.	25		
	Think of two different four- or five-digit mystery numbers. Write clues for your classmates to try to discover each number. Be creative when you use place value in your clues.	25		
	Total number of points you are planning to earn from Side 1.	**Total points earned from Side 1:**		

Name: _____   ▲

Place Value: Side 2

Guidelines:

1. You may complete as many of the activities listed within the time period.
2. You may choose any combination of activities.
3. Your goal is 100 points. You may earn up to _____ points extra credit.
4. You may be as creative as you like within the guidelines listed below.
5. You must show your plan to your teacher by _____.
6. Activities may be turned in at any time during the working time period. They will be graded and recorded on this sheet as you continue to work, so keep it safe!

Plan to Do	Activity to Complete (Side 2: 30–35 points)	Point Value	Date Completed	Points Earned
	Perform a song or rap about numbers in the thousands, millions, and billions.	30		
	Read the book *How Much Is a Million?* Choose your own item and calculate how much space it would take to reach a million.	35		
	If you had a million dollars to spend, what would you buy? Create a list with the cost of each item showing how you would spend the money.	35		
	Research the names of numbers over one billion. Create a scrapbook that contains examples of things that might be counted with such large numbers.	35		
	Using the scale on a world map, create a PowerPoint presentation that tells about five well-known places: one that is about 1,000 miles from your home, one that is 2,000 miles away, and three that are more than 3,000 miles. Be sure to include exactly how far away each location is!	35		
	Free choice: must be outlined on a proposal form and approved before beginning work.	10–40 points		
	Total number of points you are planning to earn from Side 1.	**Total points earned from Side 1:**		
	Total number of points you are planning to earn from Side 2.	**Total points earned from Side 2:**		
		Grand Total (/100)		

I am planning to complete _____ activities that could earn up to a total of _____ points.

Teacher's initials _____ Student's signature _____

Place Value: Side 1

Guidelines:

1. You may complete as many of the activities listed within the time period.
2. You may choose any combination of activities.
3. Your goal is 100 points. You may earn up to _____ points extra credit.
4. You may be as creative as you like within the guidelines listed below.
5. You must show your plan to your teacher by _____.
6. Activities may be turned in at any time during the working time period. They will be graded and recorded on this sheet as you continue to work, so keep it safe!

Plan to Do	Activity to Complete (Side 1: 15–25 points)	Point Value	Date Completed	Points Earned
	Find the populations of five cities in your state. Put them in order from least to greatest.	15		
	Create a set of concentration cards with numbers and their place values to help your classmates practice.	15		
	Complete a classmate's crossword puzzle.	15		
	Create a mobile to represent the population of your state. For each number, give its place value.	15		
	Create a set of trading cards, one for each place value. Be creative in the facts you record about each.	20		
	Research the distances of the planets in the solar system from Earth. Make a chart that lists the planets and their distances in order from farthest to closest.	20		
	Design a folded quiz book about the place values we are studying.	20		
	Create a number crossword puzzle to help your classmates practice place value.	25		
	Perform a song or rap about numbers in the thousands, millions, and billions.	25		
	Total number of points you are planning to earn from Side 1.	**Total points earned from Side 1:**		

Name: _____

Place Value: Side 2

Guidelines:
1. You may complete as many of the activities listed within the time period.
2. You may choose any combination of activities.
3. Your goal is 100 points. You may earn up to _____ points extra credit.
4. You may be as creative as you like within the guidelines listed below.
5. You must show your plan to your teacher by _____.
6. Activities may be turned in at any time during the working time period. They will be graded and recorded on this sheet as you continue to work, so keep it safe!

Plan to Do	Activity to Complete (Side 2: 30–35 points)	Point Value	Date Completed	Points Earned
	If you had a million dollars to spend, what would you buy? Create a list with the cost of each item to show how you would spend the money.	30		
	Read the book *How Much Is a Million?* Choose your own item and calculate how much space it would take to reach a million.	30		
	Think of two different four- or five-digit mystery numbers. Write clues for your classmates to try to discover each number. Be creative when you use place value in your clues.	30		
	Research the names of numbers over one billion. Create a scrapbook that contains examples of things that might be counted with such large numbers.	30		
	Using the scale on a world map, create a PowerPoint presentation that tells about five well-known places: one that is about 1,000 miles from your home, one that is 2,000 miles away, and three that are more than 3,000 miles away. Be sure to include exactly how far away each location is!	35		
	Free choice: must be outlined on a proposal form and approved before beginning work.	10–40 points		
	Total number of points you are planning to earn from Side 1.	**Total points earned from Side 1:**		
	Total number of points you are planning to earn from Side 2.	**Total points earned from Side 2:**		
		Grand Total (/100)		

I am planning to complete _____ activities that could earn up to a total of _____ points.

Teacher's initials _____ Student's signature _____

Prime and Composite Numbers

2-5-8 Menus

Objectives Covered Through These Menus and These Activities
- Students will distinguish between prime and composite numbers.
- Students will identify examples of prime and composite numbers in the world around them.

Materials Needed by Students for Completion
- 100s charts
- Newspapers (sports, business, and weather sections)
- Magazines (for collages) ▲
- Large index cards (for rule cards)
- Instructions for making a dichotomous key (p. 60)

Special Notes on the Use of These Menus
These menus offer the option to create a dichotomous key. Some students may not have had experience creating one. Included is an instruction sheet with examples, but the key students create will be much more detailed.

Time Frame
- 1–2 weeks—Students are given the menus as the unit is started, and the teacher discusses all of the product options on the menus. As the different options are discussed, students will choose products that add to a total of 10 points. As the lessons progress through the week, the teacher and the students should refer back to the options associated with the content being taught.
- 1–2 days—The teacher chooses an activity from the menus to use with the entire class.

Suggested Forms
- All-purpose rubric
- Point-based free-choice proposal form ▲

Prime and Composite Numbers

Directions: Choose at least two activities from the menu below. The activities must total at least 10 points. Place a check mark next to each box to show which activities you will complete. All activities must be completed by: _____.

---

2 Points

☐ Fill in a 100s chart. Color code the prime and composite numbers.

☐ Create a collage of prime and composite numbers that you have located in magazines. Include at least 10 prime and 10 composite numbers, and label each number.

---

5 Points

☐ Select an article that has a lot of numbers in it from the sports or weather section of the newspaper. Go through the article and circle all of the composite numbers and place a square around all of the prime numbers.

☐ Create a rule card that lists all of the ways to check if a large number is prime or composite.

☐ Create a song or rap that would help your classmates remember the difference between prime and composite numbers.

☐ Free choice—Submit a free-choice proposal form to your teacher for approval.

---

8 Points

☐ Write a journal entry about either a prime or a composite number and its feelings about its fact families.

☐ Crisis has struck. The number 8 has suddenly disappeared. All of the numbers in its fact family, as well as the numbers it is a part of, have gotten together to try to search for it. Make an attendance list that tells the relationship to 8 of all of the numbers that will join the search.

Prime and Composite Numbers

Directions: Choose at least two activities from the menu below. The activities must total at least 10 points. Place a check mark next to each box to show which activities you will complete. All activities must be completed by: _____.

---

2 Points

❐ Fill in a 100s chart. Color code the prime and composite numbers.

❐ Select an article that has a lot of numbers in it from the sports or weather section of the newspaper. Go through the article and circle all of the composite numbers and place a square around all of the prime numbers.

---

5 Points

❐ Write a journal entry about either a prime or a composite number and its feelings about its fact families.

❐ Create a rule card that lists all of the ways to check if a large number is prime or composite.

❐ Create a song or rap that would help your classmates remember the difference between prime and composite numbers.

❐ Design an advertisement for composite or prime numbers, focusing on specific numbers and their uses.

---

8 Points

❐ Create your own dichotomous key or flow chart that tells the steps for determining if a number is prime or composite. Try to find the fewest steps to guarantee your answer.

❐ Crisis has struck. The number 8 has suddenly disappeared. All of the numbers in its fact family, as well as the numbers it is a part of, have gotten together to try and search for it. Make an attendance list that tells the relationship to 8 of all of the numbers that will join the search.

How to Make a Dichotomous Key

Dichotomous keys are designed to ask questions of the user and eventually lead to a final answer as the user makes decisions. There are different ways to organize these questions. They can be designed in a flow chart design or be a simple list of questions. In order to design a dichotomous key, you want to start asking questions from broad to specific, so users will find their answers.

Let's say that a group of high school students have come to present a play for your class and you do not know their names. A dichotomous key would help you discover their names based on what you observe about the students. Below are two different examples of the same information in the two different kinds of keys. Using the information in the dichotomous keys, see if you can figure out the name of each high school student.

Dichotomous Keys: Flow Chart

The following page shows an example of a dichotomous key flow chart. This type of key uses arrows, which allow the user to follow a path to an unknown object. You would start with the very general question: Is the unknown person a boy or girl? If he is a boy, you will continue on the "boy" path to try and discover the name of the group member. If the person is a girl, your path is a lot shorter. This group only has one girl.

Dichotomous Keys: Question List

This type of key asks questions to help students try and identify an unknown object. The first question is very general

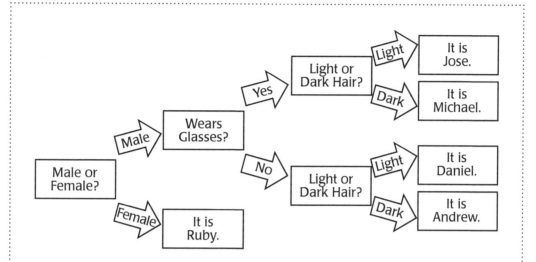

and usually splits the group into two smaller groups. For this key, you will want to know first if the student you are trying to identify is a boy or a girl. From that point on, the questions get more specific.

1. Is the unknown person male or female? If male, go to 2. If female, go to 6.
2. Male: Does he wear glasses? If yes, go to 3. If no, go to 4.
3. Does he have light or dark hair? If light, go to 8. If dark, go to 9.
4. Does he have light or dark hair? If light, go to 5. If dark, go to 7.
5. It is Daniel.
6. It is Ruby.
7. It is Andrew.
8. It is Jose.
9. It is Michael.

How did you do with your identification of the students?

Coordinate Graphs

2-5-8 Menus

Objectives Covered Through These Menus and These Activities
- Students will plot points on a coordinate graph.
- Students will understand uses for coordinate graphs in our daily lives.

Materials Needed by Students for Completion
- Poster board or large white paper
- Graph paper
- Materials for board games (folders, colored cards, etc.)
- Magazines (for collages)
- Large index cards (for instruction cards)
- Coat hangers (for mobiles)
- Index cards (for mobiles)
- String (for mobiles)
- Different maps, including state maps

Special Notes on the Use of These Menus
Two of the activities call for students to use local and state maps. These can usually be obtained free of charge through a local travel bureau or a local AAA agency.

Time Frame
- 1–2 weeks—Students are given the menus as the unit is started, and the teacher discusses all of the product options on the menus. As the different options are discussed, students will choose products that add to a total of 10 points. As the lessons progress through the week, the teacher and the students should refer back to the options associated with the content being taught.
- 1–2 days—The teacher chooses an activity from the menus to use with the entire class.

Suggested Forms
- All-purpose rubric

Coordinate Graphs

Directions: Choose at least two activities from the menu below. The activities must total at least 10 points. Place a check mark next to each box to show which activities you will complete. All activities must be completed by: _____.

2 Points

- ☐ Design a mobile that shows at least five points and their locations on graphs.
- ☐ Create an instruction card that tells how to read a graph and how to graph points.

5 Points

- ☐ Using a piece of graph paper, make a drawing. Write instructions telling how to have other students create your drawing using only coordinates.
- ☐ Create a brochure that shows how to plot points and read coordinate graphs.
- ☐ Create a poster that shows at least five uses of coordinate graphs in our daily lives.
- ☐ Develop a game that you could play with friends. It has to have coordinates that are used to move forward in the game.

8 Points

- ☐ Maps are divided into areas. You can use the coordinates labeled to find different cities. After examining different maps, make a map of your school and playground with different points of interest and their coordinates. List the points and their locations in a legend.
- ☐ Design a collage of pictures. Place a coordinate graph over the pictures. Create a worksheet that asks your classmates about the locations of different items on your collage.

Coordinate Graphs

Directions: Choose at least two activities from the menu below. The activities must total at least 10 points. Place a check mark next to each box to show which activities you will complete. All activities must be completed by: _____.

---

2 Points
☐ Create a brochure that shows how to plot points and how to read coordinate graphs.

☐ Create an instruction card that tells how to read a graph and how to graph points.

---

5 Points
☐ Using a piece of graph paper, make a drawing. Write instructions telling other students how to create your drawing using only coordinates.

☐ Develop a game that you could play with friends. It has to have coordinates that are used to move forward in the game.

☐ Create a poster that shows at least five uses of coordinate graphs in our daily lives.

☐ Design a collage of pictures. Place a coordinate graph over the pictures. Create a worksheet that asks your classmates about the locations of different items on your collage.

---

8 Points
☐ Maps are divided into areas. You can use the coordinates labeled to find different cities. After examining different maps, make a map of your school and playground with different points of interest and their coordinates. List the points and their locations in a legend.

☐ Design a scavenger hunt on your state map. Make up fun questions and riddles that can only be answered by visiting the coordinates you include in the hunt. Be creative when designing your scavenger hunt. Challenge your classmates to find at least 15 items.

Money

Three Shape Menu ▲ and Tic-Tac-Toe Menu ●

Objectives Covered Through These Menus and These Activities
- Students will create different combinations of coins.
- Students will complete calculations with money.
- Students will analyze the saving and spending of money in everyday situations.

Materials Needed by Students for Completion
- Poster board or large white paper
- Materials for board games (folders, colored cards, etc.) ●
- Coat hangers (for mobiles)
- Index cards (for mobiles)
- String (for mobiles)
- Scrapbooking materials ▲
- Catalogs or Internet shopping sites
- Materials for student-created models

Special Notes on the Use of These Menus
This topic has two different menu formats: Three Shape menu and Tic-Tac-Toe menu. The Three Shape menu is specifically selected for the triangle (lower level) option, as it easily allows the menu to be broken into manageable bits. The menu itself can be cut into strips of the same shape. Students can then be given a strip of square product choices for their use. Once they have chosen and submitted the square product for grading, they can be given the circle strip, and lastly, they can complete the diamond strip. Because this type of menu is designed to become more advanced as students move through the shapes, teachers may choose to provide their students who have special needs with the top two shapes and save the diamonds for enrichment.

Time Frame
- 2 weeks—Students are given the menus as the unit is started. The teacher will go over all of the options for that content and have students note the activities they are most interested in completing. As the teacher presents lessons throughout the week, he or she should

refer back to the options associated with that content. If students are using the Tic-Tac-Toe menu form, completed products should make a column or a row. If students are using the Three Shape menu form, they should complete one product from each different shape group. When students complete these patterns, they will have completed one activity from three different objectives, learning styles, or levels of Bloom's Revised taxonomy. When students make these patterns, they will have completed one activity on budgeting money, one activity on change and different coin combinations, and one problem-solving activity using money.

- 1 week—At the start of the unit, the teacher chooses the three activities he or she feels are most valuable for the students. Stations can be set up in the classroom. These three activities are available for student choice throughout the week, as regular instruction takes place.
- 1–2 days—The teacher chooses an activity from the menus to use with the entire class.

Suggested Forms

- All-purpose rubric
- Free-choice proposal form ●

Name: _____   ▲

Money

Directions: Choose one activity from each shape group. Circle one choice from each group of shapes. Color in the shape after you have finished it. All activities must be completed by: _____.

Your sister has been saving money for a year. She wants to trade it in for dollar bills. Create a poster to show her the different combinations of coins that can make $1.

Design a $1 mind map that shows at least 10 combinations of coins that can add up to $1.

Make a scrapbook of items that cost less than $20 each. For each item, show a picture, its cost, and the change you would receive if you paid for it with a $20 bill.

Every year, your aunt gives you $10 times your age. If you save all of this money, will you have enough for a car once you get your driver's license? Show your work.

Each time players on a game show answer a question correctly, their money doubles. Make a mobile to show how they can become millionaires if they start with just $1.

Mr. Monie must pay his electric bill of $72 with only nickels and pennies. Propose two options for how he can pay his bill.

Your parents have given you a budget of $200 to invite, feed, and entertain your friends for a birthday party. Develop a budget for your party.

A machine that counts your change charges 9 cents on the dollar. Is this service worth it? Create a brochure with examples of calculations on the advantages and disadvantages.

You are redesigning your bedroom. List the items you would like, create a model of how you want your room to look, and total the amount of money it will cost.

67

Name: _____

Money

Directions: Check the boxes you plan to complete. They should form a tic-tac-toe across or down. All products are due by: _____.

☐ *The Next Sensation?* You have a great idea for a new board game. It will be based on saving and spending money, and it will even have a bank. Develop this game and bring it to class for your classmates to play.	☐ *Thanks, Aunt Kay!* For your birthday each year, one of your relatives has decided to give you $10 times your age that year (e.g., $50 for your fifth birthday). If all of this money goes into your savings account, will you be able to afford a car by the time you get your driver's license? Perform a play to show your results.	☐ *Combinations of Money* Your little sister has been saving her money for a year now. She wants to take it all to the bank and trade it in for dollar bills. Create a poster to show her all of the different combinations of coins that could make $1.
☐ *Change Counting Machines* There are machines that will count your change for you, but they charge a fee of 9 cents on the dollar. Is this fee worth it? What is the minimum number of coins you would turn in (how many coins do you think this fee would be worth paying for)? Create a brochure on the advantages and disadvantages of these machines. Include specific examples and calculations.	☐ **Free Choice** (Fill out your proposal form before beginning the free choice!)	☐ *The Perfect Party* Your parents have promised you a fabulous birthday party. However, you must be able to invite, feed, and entertain all of your friends for less than $200. Develop your plan for having your party and staying within the budget.
☐ *Combinations of Money* Mr. Monie has been saving change his entire life. The time has come for him to pay his electric bill this month, and he doesn't have any dollar bills. He decides he wouldn't mind spending nickels and pennies, but nothing else. If his electric bill is $78, propose two options for him to pay his bill.	☐ *My Perfect Bedroom* Your parents are allowing you to redesign your room. Make a list of all of the items you would like to have. Create a model that shows how you would like it to look, and total the amount of money that it would take to create your perfect bedroom.	☐ *Winning Millions?* You have created a television show in which participants can win money based on answering questions correctly. Each time they answer a question correctly, their money doubles. If they start with just $1, how many questions will they need to answer correctly to be millionaires? Prepare a mobile that shows participants how they can win a million dollars.

Adding and Subtracting Decimals

2-5-8 Menus

Objectives Covered Through These Menus and These Activities
- Students will add and subtract decimals.
- Students will give examples of decimals in the real world.

Materials Needed by Students for Completion
- Poster board or large white paper
- Access to library books (classified under the Dewey Decimal System)
- Microsoft PowerPoint or other slideshow software
- Newspapers
- Take-out or online restaurant menus with prices
- Blank index cards (for concentration card games)

Special Notes on the Use of These Menus
These menus contain an activity that will require the support of the school librarian. The students are asked to find all of the books in the library about a certain topic and add their Dewey Decimal System numbers together. If time is a consideration, the librarian could pull certain books that focus on math and have them placed in a special spot in the library so students can easily locate them and record their numbers.

Time Frame
- 1–2 weeks—Students are given the menus as the unit is started, and the teacher discusses all of the product options on the menus. As the different options are discussed, students will choose products that add to a total of 10 points. As the lessons progress through the week, the teacher and the students should refer back to the options associated with the content being taught.
- 1–2 days—The teacher chooses an activity from the menus to use with the entire class.

Suggested Forms
- All-purpose rubric
- Point-based free-choice proposal form

Adding and Subtracting Decimals

Directions: Choose at least two activities from the menu below. The activities must total at least 10 points. Place a check mark next to each box to show which activities you will complete. All activities must be completed by: _____.

---

2 Points
- ❏ Create a worksheet for your classmates to help them practice adding and subtracting decimals.
- ❏ Create a flipbook with examples of adding and subtracting decimals on the flaps with the answers inside.

---

5 Points
- ❏ Create a concentration card game to match decimal word problems with their answers.
- ❏ Decimals are big news! Go through two sections of your newspaper and locate all of the numbers recorded as decimals. Estimate the total of all of the numbers, and then calculate it.
- ❏ Using a restaurant menu, create a dinner order for a family of four. Each should have a drink and a main dish. Appetizers and desserts are optional. You should spend as close to $70 as possible. Create a poster to show your dinner order and how much each item will cost.
- ❏ Free choice—Prepare a proposal form and submit it to your teacher for approval.

---

8 Points
- ❏ Choose a sport. Prepare a PowerPoint presentation that explains how statistics are calculated for that sport. Share examples in your explanation.
- ❏ Library books can be located by the Dewey decimal numbers on their spines. Just for fun, your school librarian has offered a prize for the first student who can tell her the total of all of the Dewey decimal numbers on the books about animals. A student has turned in the answer, but you have been given the assignment of checking the answer. On a poster, show the books you have found and how you calculated the correct answer.

Adding and Subtracting Decimals

Directions: Choose at least two activities from the menu below. The activities must total at least 10 points. Place a check mark next to each box to show which activities you will complete. All activities must be completed by:_____.

2 Points

❐ Create a worksheet for your classmates to help them practice adding and subtracting decimals.

❐ Create a flipbook with examples of adding and subtracting decimals on the flaps with the answers inside.

5 Points

❐ Create a concentration card game to match decimal word problems with their answers.

❐ Decimals are big news! Go through two sections of your newspaper and locate all of the numbers recorded as decimals. Estimate the total of all of the numbers, and then calculate it.

❐ Library books can be located by the Dewey decimal numbers on their spines. Just for fun, your school librarian has offered a prize for the first student who can tell her the total of all of the Dewey decimal numbers on the books about weather. A student has turned in the answer, but you have been given the assignment of checking the answer. On a poster, show the books you have found and how you calculated the correct answer.

❐ Using a restaurant menu, create a dinner order for a family of four. Each should have a drink and a main dish. Appetizers and desserts are optional. You should spend as close to $70 as possible. Create a poster to show your dinner order and how much each item will cost.

8 Points

❐ Choose a sport. Prepare a PowerPoint presentation that explains how statistics are calculated for that sport. Share examples in your explanation.

❐ Free choice—Prepare a proposal form and submit it to your teacher for approval.

Decimals

List Menus

Objectives Covered Through These Menus and These Activities
- Students will multiply and divide decimals.
- Students will add and subtract decimals.
- Students will show real-world examples of calculations with decimals.
- Students will identify relationships between fractions and decimals.

Materials Needed by Students for Completion
- Graph paper or Internet access (for crossword puzzles)
- Cube template
- Microsoft PowerPoint or other slideshow software
- Large index cards (for instruction cards)
- Recipes from recipe books
- Blank index cards (for card games, trading cards, and concentration cards)

Time Frame
- 1–2 weeks—Students are given the menus as the unit is started and the guidelines and point expectations on the menus are discussed. Because these menus cover one topic in depth, the teacher will go over all of the options for the topic being covered and have students place check marks in the boxes next to the activities they are most interested in completing. As instruction continues, the activities are completed by students and submitted for grading.
- 1–2 days—The teacher chooses an activity from an objective to use with the entire class during the lesson time.

Suggested Forms
- All-purpose rubric
- Point-based free-choice proposal form

Name: _____ ▲

Decimals: Side 1

Guidelines:
1. You may complete as many of the activities listed within the time period.
2. You may choose any combination of activities.
3. Your goal is 100 points. You may earn up to _____ points extra credit.
4. You may be as creative as you like within the guidelines listed below.
5. You must show your plan to your teacher by _____.
6. Activities may be turned in at any time during the working time period. They will be graded and recorded on this sheet as you continue to work, so keep it safe!

Plan to Do	Activity to Complete (Side 1: 15–25 points)	Point Value	Date Completed	Points Earned
	Create an instruction card that shows the steps for adding, subtracting, multiplying, and dividing decimals.	15		
	Design a worksheet to help your classmates practice calculations with decimals.	20		
	Create a set of trading cards for all of the decimals in the eighths family. Include their equivalent fractions, facts about them, and at least one drawing.	25		
	Make a Venn diagram to compare and contrast decimals and fractions.	25		
	Create a set of concentration cards to match decimals with their equivalent fractions.	25		
	Create a book cover for a math book entitled *Decimals in Our Daily Lives*.	25		
	Create a project cube with real-world examples of adding, subtracting, multiplying, and dividing decimals.	25		
	Write a letter to your parents about how decimals are part of our daily lives. Include examples to prove your point.	25		
	Total number of points you are planning to earn from Side 1.	**Total points earned from Side 1:**		

Name: _____ ▲

Decimals: Side 2

Guidelines:
1. You may complete as many of the activities listed within the time period.
2. You may choose any combination of activities.
3. Your goal is 100 points. You may earn up to _____ points extra credit.
4. You may be as creative as you like within the guidelines listed below.
5. You must show your plan to your teacher by _____.
6. Activities may be turned in at any time during the working time period. They will be graded and recorded on this sheet as you continue to work, so keep it safe!

Plan to Do	Activity to Complete (Side 2: 30–45 points)	Point Value	Date Completed	Points Earned
	Convert one of your favorite recipes from fractions into decimals. If you needed to prepare the recipe for your class, how much of each ingredient would you need?	30		
	Create a PowerPoint presentation that shows how to add, subtract, multiply, and divide decimals.	30		
	Design a brochure that discusses all of the different places we see decimals and fractions every day.	30		
	Create a decimal crossword puzzle in which all of the answers are written in words and all of the clues are problems.	35		
	Create a cube game using three cubes. In this game, the players will roll two dice to get decimal numbers and one die to get the mathematical function they must complete. Provide an answer card for all of the possible combinations.	35		
	Create a number path starting with the number 11.42 and ending with the number 36.41. Your path must have at least seven steps and must include addition, subtraction, and multiplication. Show your path on a poster.	45		
	Free choice: must be outlined on a proposal form and approved before beginning work.	10–40 points		
	Total number of points you are planning to earn from Side 1.	**Total points earned from Side 1:**		
	Total number of points you are planning to earn from Side 2.	**Total points earned from Side 2:**		
		Grand Total (/100)		

I am planning to complete _____ activities that could earn up to a total of _____ points.

Teacher's initials _____ Student's signature _____

74

Name: _____   ●

Decimals: Side 1

Guidelines:

1. You may complete as many of the activities listed within the time period.
2. You may choose any combination of activities.
3. Your goal is 100 points. You may earn up to _____ points extra credit.
4. You may be as creative as you like within the guidelines listed below.
5. You must show your plan to your teacher by _____.
6. Activities may be turned in at any time during the working time period. They will be graded and recorded on this sheet as you continue to work, so keep it safe!

Plan to Do	Activity to Complete (Side 1: 15–25 points)	Point Value	Date Completed	Points Earned
	Create an instruction card that shows the steps for adding, subtracting, multiplying, and dividing decimals.	15		
	Create a project cube with real-world examples of adding, subtracting, multiplying, and dividing decimals.	20		
	Convert one of your favorite recipes from fractions into decimals. If you needed to prepare the recipe for your class, how much of each ingredient would you need?	25		
	Make a Venn diagram to compare and contrast decimals and fractions.	25		
	Create a book cover for a math book entitled *Decimals in Our Daily Lives.*	25		
	Create a PowerPoint presentation that shows how to add, subtract, multiply, and divide decimals.	25		
	Create a set of trading cards for all of the decimals in the eighths family. Include their equivalent fractions, facts about them, and at least one drawing.	25		
	Write a letter to your parents about how decimals are part of our daily lives. Include examples to prove your point.	25		
	Total number of points you are planning to earn from Side 1.	**Total points earned from Side 1:**		

Name: _____

Decimals: Side 2

Guidelines:

1. You may complete as many of the activities listed within the time period.
2. You may choose any combination of activities.
3. Your goal is 100 points. You may earn up to _____ points extra credit.
4. You may be as creative as you like within the guidelines listed below.
5. You must show your plan to your teacher by _____.
6. Activities may be turned in at any time during the working time period. They will be graded and recorded on this sheet as you continue to work, so keep it safe!

Plan to Do	Activity to Complete (Side 2: 30–35 points)	Point Value	Date Completed	Points Earned
	Create a cube game using three cubes. In this game, the players will roll two dice to get decimal numbers and one die to get the mathematical function they must complete. Provide an answer card for all of the possible combinations.	30		
	Design a brochure that discusses all of the different places we see decimals and fractions every day.	35		
	Create a decimal crossword puzzle in which all of the clues are problems and all of the answers are written in words.	35		
	Create a number path starting with the number 15.23 and ending with the number 40.41. Your path must have at least seven steps and must include addition, subtraction, and multiplication. Show your path on a poster.	35		
	Free choice: must be outlined on a proposal form and approved before beginning work.	10–40 points		
	Total number of points you are planning to earn from Side 1.	**Total points earned from Side 1:**		
	Total number of points you are planning to earn from Side 2.	**Total points earned from Side 2:**		
		Grand Total (/100)		

I am planning to complete _____ activities that could earn up to a total of _____ points.

Teacher's initials _____ Student's signature _____

Decimals Cube

Complete the cube for decimals. Each side of the cube should show real-world examples of adding, subtracting, multiplying, and dividing decimals. Use this pattern or create your own cube.

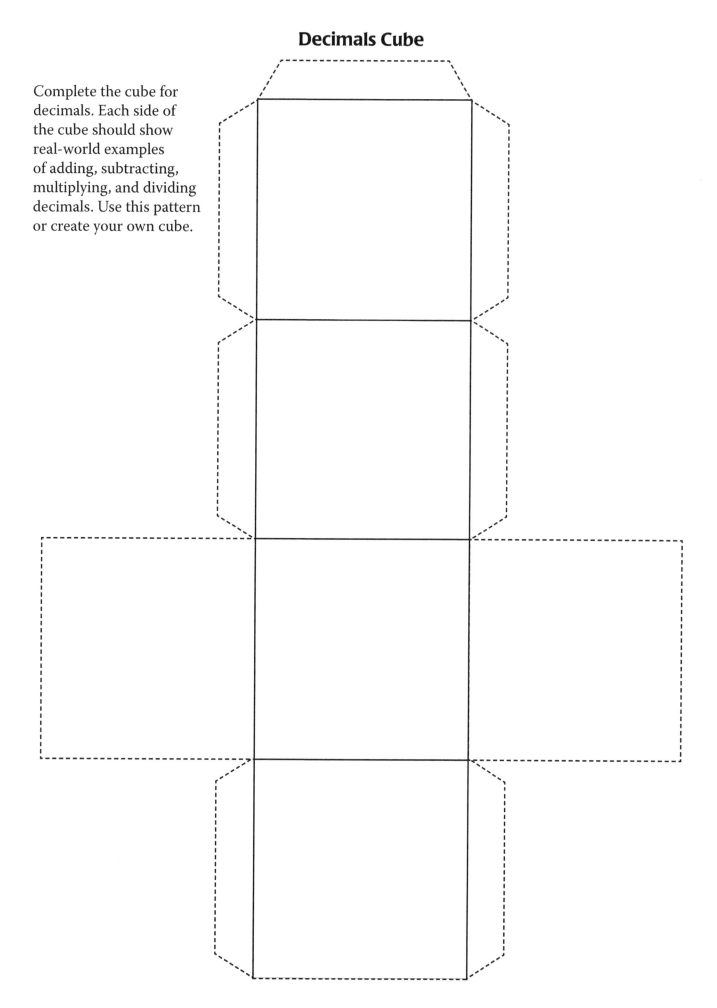

Whole Numbers

List Menu ▲ and Baseball Menu ●

Objectives Covered Through These Menus and These Activities
- Students will add and subtract whole numbers.
- Students will multiply and divide whole numbers.
- Students will solve problems with whole numbers.
- Students will show how mathematics is used in our daily lives.

Materials Needed by Students for Completion
- Poster board or large white paper
- Graph paper or Internet access (for crossword puzzles)
- Materials for board games (folders, colored cards, etc.)
- Microsoft PowerPoint or other slideshow software ●
- Blank index cards (for concentration cards and trading cards)
- Cube template
- Materials for student-created lessons
- Advertisements from local grocery stores
- Video camera (for educational videos)

Special Notes on the Use of These Menus
This topic has two different menu formats: List menu and Baseball menu. Two different formats were selected based on the comfort levels of the students. The Baseball menu can seem overwhelming to special needs students, so similar activities and point values have been used on the List menu; this often makes such a large number of options seem more manageable.

These menus allow students to create their own educational videos. You may want to plan class time for activity work on this menu, or these students may need to schedule extra time with you to get the videos completed on time.

Time Frame
- 1–2 weeks—Students are given the menus as the unit is started and the guidelines and point expectations on the top of the menus are discussed. Usually, students are expected to complete 100 points. Because these menus cover one topic in depth, the teacher will go

over all of the options for the topic being covered and have students place check marks in the boxes next to the activities they are most interested in completing. As instruction continues, the activities are completed by students and submitted for grading.

- 1–2 days—The teacher chooses an activity from an objective to use with the entire class during the lesson time.

Suggested Forms

- All-purpose rubric
- Student presentation rubric
- Point-based free-choice form ▲

Whole Numbers: Side 1

Guidelines:

1. You may complete as many of the activities listed within the time period.
2. You may choose any combination of activities.
3. Your goal is 100 points. You may earn up to _____ points extra credit.
4. You may be as creative as you like within the guidelines listed below.
5. You must show your plan to your teacher by _____.
6. Activities may be turned in at any time during the working time period. They will be graded and recorded on this sheet as you continue to work, so keep it safe!

Plan to Do	Activity to Complete (Side 1: 15–30 points)	Point Value	Date Completed	Points Earned
	Create a set of concentration cards for appropriate multiplication and division facts.	15		
	Design an instructional poster that shows the steps for completing complex addition, subtraction, multiplication, and division problems.	15		
	Count the number of students in your class, and develop six word problems involving the number of students. Submit the problems and the solutions, showing all of your work.	15		
	Design a worksheet to have your classmates practice working with whole numbers.	15		
	Create a set of four trading cards: one each for multiplication, division, addition, and subtraction.	20		
	Create a mathematical crossword puzzle in which the clues are the problems.	25		
	Create a cube with a different word problem on each side.	25		
	Write a children's storybook about the number 8 and what happens to it when it gets added, subtracted, multiplied, and divided.	30		
	Total number of points you are planning to earn from Side 1.	**Total points earned from Side 1:**		

Name: _____ ▲

Whole Numbers: Side 2

Guidelines:

1. You may complete as many of the activities listed within the time period.
2. You may choose any combination of activities.
3. Your goal is 100 points. You may earn up to _____ points extra credit.
4. You may be as creative as you like within the guidelines listed below.
5. You must show your plan to your teacher by _____.
6. Activities may be turned in at any time during the working time period. They will be graded and recorded on this sheet as you continue to work, so keep it safe!

Plan to Do	Activity to Complete (Side 2: 35–100 points)	Point Value	Date Completed	Points Earned
	Create a brochure about how mathematics is used in our everyday lives.	35		
	Make a board game to reinforce multiplication and division problem-solving skills.	35		
	Create a song that shares the steps to solve a math problem using two-digit numbers.	40		
	Create a commercial that explains why multiplication is important in our everyday lives.	40		
	You have been given the task of creating a shopping list that would supply enough food to feed your family for a week. Using the advertisements from the local grocery stores, develop your plan. You should plan on spending no more than $35 per person in your family. Make a report that shares the specific costs of your plan.	60		
	Write a 1–2-page story using numbers, and then write five word problems using information presented in the story. Your problems should be creative and complex!	60		
	Create your own Mr. or Ms. Math Video in which you teach viewers about adding, subtracting, multiplying, and dividing. Your video should present basic problems as well as word problems. It should also include at least three commercials for math-based products. Be creative and have fun!	100		
	Free choice: must be outlined on a proposal form and approved before beginning work.	10–40 points		
	Total number of points you are planning to earn from Side 1.	**Total points earned from Side 1:**		
	Total number of points you are planning to earn from Side 2.	**Total points earned from Side 2:**		
		Grand Total (/100)		

I am planning to complete _____ activities that could earn up to a total of _____ points.

Teacher's initials _____ Student's signature _____

Whole Numbers

Look through the following choices and decide how you want to make your game add to **100 points**. Singles are worth 10, Doubles are worth 30, Triples are worth 50, and Homeruns are worth 100. Choose any combination you want! Place a **check mark** next to each choice you are going to complete. Make sure that your points equal 100!

Singles—10 Points Each

- ❒ Create a set of concentration cards for appropriate multiplication and division facts.
- ❒ Count the number of students in your class, and develop six word problems involving the number of students. Submit the problems and the solutions, showing all of your work.
- ❒ Design an instructional poster that shows the steps for completing complex addition, subtraction, multiplication, and division problems.
- ❒ Create a mathematical crossword puzzle in which the clues are problems.
- ❒ Design a worksheet to have your classmates practice working with whole numbers.
- ❒ Create a set of four trading cards: one each for multiplication, division, addition, and subtraction.

Doubles—30 Points Each

- ❒ Create a brochure about how mathematics is used in our everyday lives.
- ❒ Create a song that shares the steps for solving a math problem using two-digit numbers.
- ❒ Create a cube with a different word problem on each side.
- ❒ Complete two Venn diagrams. One will compare and contrast addition and multiplication, and the other will compare and contrast subtraction and division.
- ❒ Make a board game to reinforce multiplication and division problem-solving skills.
- ❒ Create a commercial that explains why multiplication is important in our everyday lives.

Name: _____

Triples—50 Points Each

❑ You have been given the task of creating a shopping list that would supply enough food to feed your family for a week. Using the advertisements from the local grocery stores, develop your plan. You should plan on spending no more than $35 per person in your family. Make a report that shares the specific costs of your plan.

❑ Research at least five careers that use mathematics (and whole numbers) on a daily basis. Create a PowerPoint presentation that tells about each career and how it uses mathematics. Include a specific example of the mathematics for each career.

❑ Write a 1–2-page story using numbers, and then write five word problems using information presented in the story. Your problems should be creative and complex!

Homeruns—100 Points Each

❑ Create your own Mr. or Ms. Math Video in which you teach viewers about adding, subtracting, multiplying, and dividing. Your video should present basic problems as well as word problems. It should also include at least three commercials for math-based products. Be creative and have fun!

I Chose:

_____ Singles (10 points each)

_____ Doubles (30 points each)

_____ Triples (50 points each)

_____ Homerun (100 points)

CHAPTER 6

Fractions

 DOI: 10.4324/9781003234241-6

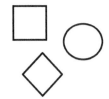

Basic Fractions

Three Shape Menu ▲ and Tic-Tac-Toe Menu ●

Objectives Covered Through These Menus and These Activities
- Students will name fractions.
- Students will place fractions in order.
- Students will show equivalent fractions.

Materials Needed by Students for Completion
- Poster board or large white paper
- Graph paper or Internet access (for crossword puzzles)
- Materials for student-created models ●
- Video camera (for how-to videos and commercials)
- Materials for board games (folders, colored cards, etc.)
- Blank index cards (for concentration cards)
- Cube template
- Recipe books

Special Notes on the Use of These Menus
This topic has two different menu formats: Three Shape menu and Tic-Tac-Toe menu. The Three Shape menu is specifically selected for the triangle (lower level) option, as it easily allows the menu to be broken into manageable bits. The menu itself can be cut into strips of the same shape. Students can then be given a strip of square product choices for their use. Once they have chosen and submitted the square product for grading, they can be given the circle strip, and lastly, they can complete the diamond strip. Because this type of menu is designed to become more advanced as students move through the shapes, teachers may choose to provide their students who have special needs with the top two shapes and save the diamonds for enrichment.

Time Frame
- 2 weeks—Students are given the menus as the unit is started. The teacher will go over all of the options for that content and have students note the activities they are most interested in completing. As the teacher presents lessons throughout the week, he or she should refer back to the options associated with that content. If students are

using the Tic-Tac-Toe menu form, completed products should make a column or a row. If students are using the Three Shape menu form, they should complete one product from each different shape group. When students complete these patterns, they will have completed one activity from three different objectives, learning styles, or levels of Bloom's Revised taxonomy. When students complete activities in this way, they will have completed one activity from each content area: naming fractions, ordering fractions, and equivalent fractions.

- 1 week—At the start of the unit, the teacher chooses the three activities he or she feels are most valuable for the students. Stations can be set up in the classroom. These three activities are available for student choice throughout the week, as regular instruction takes place.
- 1–2 days—The teacher chooses an activity from the menus to use with the entire class.

Suggested Forms

- All-purpose rubric
- Free-choice proposal form ●

Basic Fractions

Directions: Choose one activity from each shape group. Circle one choice from each group of shapes. Color in the shape after you have finished it. All activities must be completed by: _____.

Using one of your favorite recipes, convert all of the information (including the ingredient list) into a pictures-only recipe. You cannot use any words.

Create a crossword puzzle to help your classmates practice naming fractions.

Create a set of trading cards with pictures of fractions and their names.

Make a how-to video that would teach other students your age how to put fractions in order from least to greatest.

Create a game that tests your classmates' knowledge of putting fractions in order from greatest to least or from least to greatest. Include an answer key.

Make a poster that shows the steps students should go through to place fractions in order. Include examples.

Create a product cube for a fraction of your choice. Each side should have a different equivalent fraction for the fraction you chose.

Create a set of concentration cards for matching equivalent fractions. You can use pictures, words, or symbols.

Design a brochure that explains and gives examples of equivalent fractions. Include how we use them in our everyday lives.

Name: _____

Basic Fractions

Directions: Check the boxes you plan to complete. They should form a tic-tac-toe across or down. All products are due by: _____.

☐ *Naming Fractions* Using one of your favorite recipes, convert all of the information (including the ingredient list) into a pictures-only recipe. You cannot use any words.	☐ *Ordering Fractions* Develop a model that you can use to show or teach ordering fractions.	☐ *Equivalent Fractions* Design a brochure that explains and gives examples of equivalent fractions. Include how we use them in our everyday lives.
☐ *Equivalent Fractions* Create a product cube for a fraction of your choice. Each side should have a different equivalent fraction for the fraction you chose.	☐ **Free Choice** (Fill out your proposal form before beginning the free choice!)	☐ *Ordering Fractions* Create a game that tests your classmates' knowledge of putting fractions in order from greatest to least or least to greatest. Include an answer key.
☐ *Ordering Fractions* Make a how-to video that would teach other students your age how to put fractions in order from least to greatest.	☐ *Equivalent Fractions* Create a set of concentration cards for matching equivalent fractions. You can use pictures, words, or symbols.	☐ *Naming Fractions* Create a crossword puzzle so that your classmates can practice naming fractions.

Basic Fractions Cube

Complete the cube for a fraction of your choice. Each side should have a different equivalent fraction for the fraction you chose. Use this pattern or create your own cube.

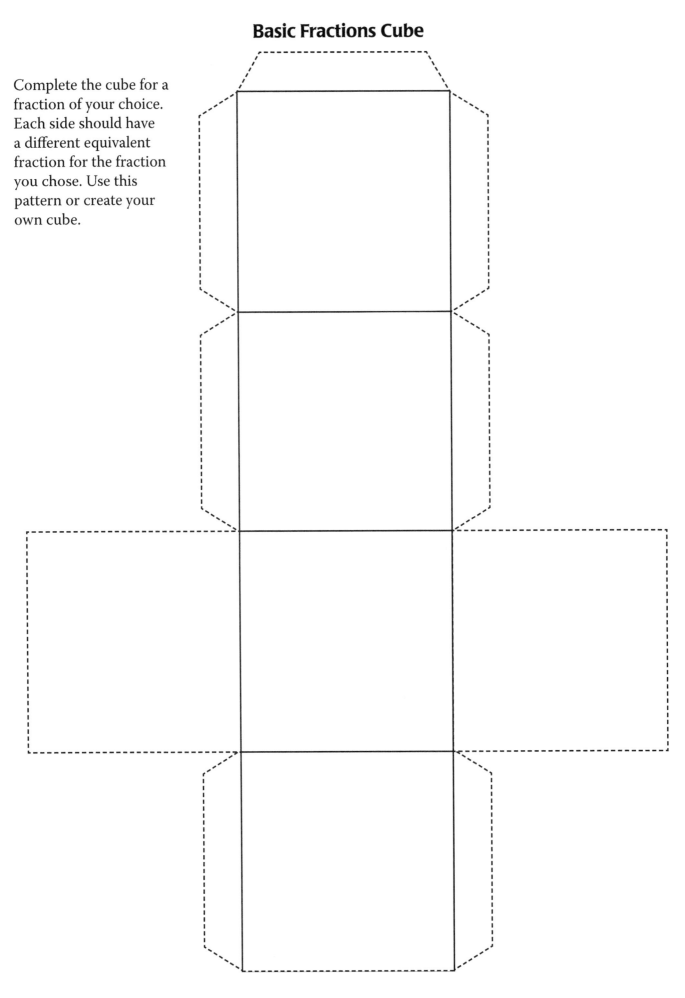

Adding and Subtracting Fractions

Three Shape Menu ▲ and Tic-Tac-Toe Menu ●

Objectives Covered Through These Menus and These Activities
- Students will add and subtract fractions.
- Students will apply the addition and subtraction of fractions to real-world situations.

Materials Needed by Students for Completion
- Poster board or large white paper
- Materials for board games (file folders, colored cards, etc.)
- Magazines
- Cube template
- Rulers
- Video camera (for commercials)
- Meter sticks or tape measures (for measuring dimensions of the classroom)

Special Notes on the Use of These Menus
Most importantly, be sure that you have enough meter sticks for the classroom measurement activity. Students really like being able to apply their knowledge to real-world situations, and having students measure the classroom for a new border is a lot of fun, but it can be distracting if class time is not planned for activity work. Students do not need to measure the top of the room (although they think they do)—they can just as easily measure around the bottom. Students can have additional fun by looking at wallpaper books obtained from home stores to propose ideas and even calculate costs for the border.

This topic has two different menu formats: Three Shape menu and Tic-Tac-Toe menu. The Three Shape menu is specifically selected for the triangle (lower level) option, as it easily allows the menu to be broken into manageable bits. The menu itself can be cut into strips of the same shape. Students can then be given a strip of square product choices for their use. Once they have chosen and submitted the square product for grading, they can be given the circle strip, and lastly, they can complete the diamond strip. Because this type of menu is designed to become more advanced as students move through the shapes, teachers may choose to provide their students who have special needs with the top two shapes and save the diamonds for enrichment.

Time Frame
- 2 weeks—Students are given the menus as the unit is started. The teacher will go over all of the options for that content and have students note the activities they are most interested in completing. As the teacher presents lessons throughout the week, he or she should refer back to the options associated with that content. If students are using the Tic-Tac-Toe menu form, completed products should make a column or a row. If students are using the Three Shape menu form, they should complete one product from each different shape group. When students complete these patterns, they will have completed one activity from three different objectives, learning styles, or levels of Bloom's Revised taxonomy.
- 1 week—At the start of the unit, the teacher chooses the three activities he or she feels are most valuable for the students. Stations can be set up in the classroom. These three activities are available for student choice throughout the week, as regular instruction takes place.
- 1–2 days—The teacher chooses an activity from the menus to use with the entire class.

Suggested Forms
- All-purpose rubric
- Free-choice proposal form ●
- Student presentation rubric

Adding and Subtracting Fractions

Directions: Choose one activity from each shape group. Circle one choice from each group of shapes. Color in the shape after you have finished it. All activities must be completed by: _____.

Create a cube with six word problems using fractions. Include three addition and three subtraction problems.

Design a worksheet where you show how to add and subtract fractions. Include some practice problems.

Using pictures from magazines, design four fraction word problems on a poster. Use the pictures to show how to complete each problem.

Make a board game that tests your classmates' knowledge of adding and subtracting fractions. Be sure to include an answer key.

Create a song or rap that tells the steps to follow when adding or subtracting fractions.

Create a windowpane showing (with an example) the steps to add and subtract fractions. Each box should have a different step, but the boxes should follow the correct order.

Create a map of your playground using a scale where every 3 feet equal ¾ of an inch. Present your map on a poster.

Your teacher needs accurate measurements down to the closest ¼ of an inch for a border to go around the classroom. Measure the room and record the length of border needed.

Create a commercial about how important adding and subtracting fractions is in our daily lives. Include one real-world example.

Name: _____

Adding and Subtracting Fractions

Directions: Check the boxes you plan to complete. They should form a tic-tac-toe across or down. All products are due by: _____.

☐ *Make a Map* Create a map of your playground using a scale where every 3 feet equals ¾ of an inch. Present your map on a poster. 	☐ *Create a Cube* Create a cube with six word problems using fractions. Include three addition and three subtraction problems.	☐ *Make a Song* Create a song or rap that tells the steps to follow when adding or subtracting fractions.  
☐ *Design a Worksheet* Design a worksheet where you show how to add and subtract fractions. Include some practice problems. 	☐ **Free Choice** (Fill out your proposal form before beginning the free choice!)	☐ *Make a Board Game* Make a board game that tests your classmates' knowledge of adding and subtracting fractions. Be sure to include an answer key. 
☐ *Create a Poster* Using pictures from magazines, design four fraction word problems on a poster. Use the pictures to show how to complete each problem.	☐ *Make a Windowpane* Create a windowpane that shows the steps for adding and subtracting fractions. Each box should have a different step, but the boxes should follow the correct order. Include an example!	☐ *Design a Border* Your teacher wants to put a new border around the classroom. Your teacher will need accurate measurements, down to the closest ⅛ of an inch. Measure your classroom and record the exact amount of border your teacher will need.

Word Problem Cube

Complete the cube for adding and subtracting fractions. Each side of the cube will include a fraction word problem. Include three addition and three subtraction problems. Use this pattern or create your own cube.

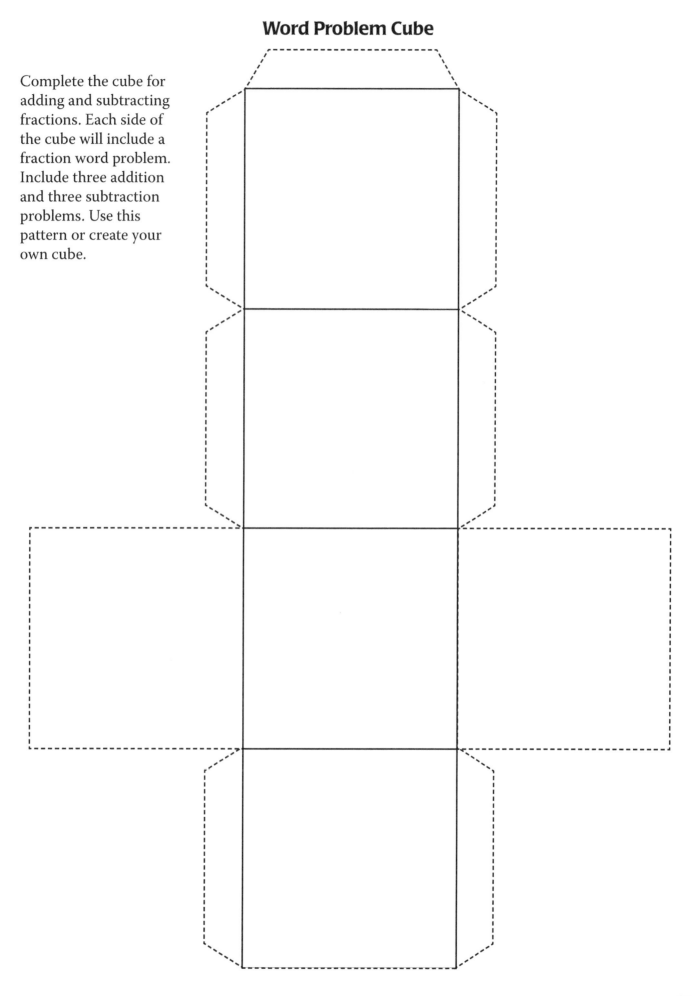

Multiplying and Dividing Fractions

List Menus

Objectives Covered Through These Menus and These Activities
- Students will multiply and divide fractions.
- Students will show examples of fractions in their daily lives.
- Students will solve problems using fractions.

Materials Needed by Students for Completion
- Graph paper or Internet access (for crossword puzzles)
- Magazines (for collages)
- Rulers (for cartoons and islands)
- Poster board or large white paper
- Materials for student models
- Recipe books
- Microsoft PowerPoint or other slideshow software
- Blank index cards (for concentration cards)

Time Frame
- 1–2 weeks—Students are given the menus as the unit is started, and the guidelines and point expectations on the menus are discussed. Because these menus cover one topic in depth, the teacher will go over all of the options for the topic being covered and have students place check marks in the boxes next to the activities they are most interested in completing. As instruction continues, the activities are completed by students and submitted for grading.
- 1–2 days—The teacher chooses an activity from an objective to use with the entire class during that lesson time.

Suggested Forms
- All-purpose rubric
- Point-based free-choice proposal form

Multiplying and Dividing Fractions: Side 1

Guidelines:

1. You may complete as many of the activities listed within the time period.
2. You may choose any combination of activities.
3. Your goal is 100 points. You may earn up to _____ points extra credit.
4. You may be as creative as you like within the guidelines listed below.
5. You must show your plan to your teacher by _____.
6. Activities may be turned in at any time during the working time period. They will be graded and recorded on this sheet as you continue to work, so keep it safe!

Plan to Do	Activity to Complete (Side 1: 15–30 points)	Point Value	Date Completed	Points Earned
	Make an "Understanding Fractions" brochure that explains how to add, subtract, multiply, and divide fractions. Include examples.	15		
	Create a set of concentration cards that match multiplication and division problems with their answers.	15		
	Complete a classmate's word problem worksheet.	15		
	Create a collage that shows various examples of using fractions in our daily lives.	20		
	Design a PowerPoint presentation that teaches students how to multiply fractions. Include various examples.	25		
	Create a number crossword puzzle for different fraction problems.	25		
	Design a worksheet with at least 10 fraction word problems. Include an answer key that shows how to solve each problem.	25		
	Create three facts and a fib about how you multiply or divide fractions.	30		
	Create an advertisement for a new machine that will complete a student's fraction problems for him or her. Explain how the machine works.	30		
	Total number of points you are planning to earn from Side 1.	**Total points earned from Side 1:**		

Multiplying and Dividing Fractions: Side 2

Guidelines:
1. You may complete as many of the activities listed within the time period.
2. You may choose any combination of activities.
3. Your goal is 100 points. You may earn up to _____ points extra credit.
4. You may be as creative as you like within the guidelines listed below.
5. You must show your plan to your teacher by _____.
6. Activities may be turned in at any time during the working time period. They will be graded and recorded on this sheet as you continue to work, so keep it safe!

Plan to Do	Activity to Complete (Side 2: 35–45 points)	Point Value	Date Completed	Points Earned
	Choose your favorite recipe. Your friends have decided to prepare it for a party of 50 people. Create a grocery list for the total number of items they will need to buy.	35		
	Create a cartoon in which the main character, One Half, has to divide itself. Be creative about why this has to happen and how it takes place.	35		
	Write a children's story about a fraction that has to keep multiplying.	35		
	Your school librarian has asked your class for help on the purchase of some new bookcases with two shelves each. She has 150 new books she needs to shelve. Half of the books are 1/2" thick. A third of them are 1/4" thick, and the rest are 3/4" thick. Her shelves are 30" long. How many bookcases should she buy? Show your work.	40		
	Draw an imaginary island on a poster. Be as creative as possible in its features. After measuring all of your island's features, create a model that is one fourth of the size of the drawing. Include a key that shows how the model dimensions were calculated.	45		
	Free choice: must be outlined on a proposal form and approved before beginning work.	10–40 points		
	Total number of points you are planning to earn from Side 1.	**Total points earned from Side 1:**		
	Total number of points you are planning to earn from Side 2.	**Total points earned from Side 2:**		
		Grand Total (/100)		

I am planning to complete _____ activities that could earn up to a total of _____ points.

Teacher's initials _____ Student's signature _____

Name:_____ •

Multiplying and Dividing Fractions: Side 1

Guidelines:
1. You may complete as many of the activities listed within the time period.
2. You may choose any combination of activities.
3. Your goal is 100 points. You may earn up to _____ points extra credit.
4. You may be as creative as you like within the guidelines listed below.
5. You must show your plan to your teacher by _____.
6. Activities may be turned in at any time during the working time period. They will be graded and recorded on this sheet as you continue to work, so keep it safe!

Plan to Do	Activity to Complete (Side 1: 15–25 points)	Point Value	Date Completed	Points Earned
	Make an "Understanding Fractions" brochure that explains how to add, subtract, multiply, and divide fractions. Include examples.	15		
	Create a collage that shows various examples of using fractions in our daily lives.	15		
	Create a set of concentration cards that match multiplication and division problems with their answers.	15		
	Complete a classmate's word problem worksheet.	15		
	Create a number crossword puzzle for different fraction problems.	20		
	Create three facts and a fib about how you multiply or divide fractions.	25		
	Create an advertisement for a new machine that will complete a student's fraction problems for him or her. Explain how the machine works.	25		
	Design a worksheet with at least 10 fraction word problems. Include an answer key that shows how to solve each problem.	25		
	Design a PowerPoint presentation that teaches students how to multiply fractions. Include various examples.	25		
	Total number of points you are planning to earn from Side 1.	**Total points earned from Side 1:**		

Name: _____

Multiplying and Dividing Fractions: Side 2

Guidelines:

1. You may complete as many of the activities listed within the time period.
2. You may choose any combination of activities.
3. Your goal is 100 points. You may earn up to _____ points extra credit.
4. You may be as creative as you like within the guidelines listed below.
5. You must show your plan to your teacher by _____.
6. Activities may be turned in at any time during the working time period. They will be graded and recorded on this sheet as you continue to work, so keep it safe!

Plan to Do	Activity to Complete (Side 2: 30–40 points)	Point Value	Date Completed	Points Earned
	Create a cartoon in which the main character, One Half, has to divide itself. Be creative about why this has to happen and how it takes place.	30		
	Choose your favorite recipe. Your friends have decided to prepare it for a party of 50 people. Create a grocery list for the total number of items they will need to buy.	30		
	Your school librarian has asked your class for help on the purchase of some new bookcases with two shelves each. She has 300 new books she needs to shelve. Half of the books are 1/2" thick. A third of them are 1/4" thick, and the rest are 3/4" thick. Her shelves are 30" long. How many bookcases should she buy? Show your work.	35		
	Write a children's story about a fraction that has to keep multiplying.	35		
	Draw an imaginary island on a poster. Be as creative as possible in creating its features. After measuring all of your island's features, create a model that is one fourth of the size of the drawing. Include a key that shows how the model dimensions were calculated.	40		
	Free choice: must be outlined on a proposal form and approved before beginning work.	10–40 points		
	Total number of points you are planning to earn from Side 1.	**Total points earned from Side 1:**		
	Total number of points you are planning to earn from Side 2.	**Total points earned from Side 2:**		
		Grand Total (/100)		

I am planning to complete _____ activities that could earn up to a total of _____ points.

Teacher's initials _____ Student's signature _____

CHAPTER 7

Probability and Statistics

 DOI: 10.4324/9781003234241-7

Using Graphs

2-5-8 Menus

Objectives Covered Through These Menus and These Activities

- Students will distinguish between different types of graphs.
- Students will read graphs and interpret the data presented.
- Students will create graphs from data.

Materials Needed by Students for Completion

- Poster board or large white paper
- Materials for student-created experiments ⬤
- Newspapers
- Coat hangers (for mobiles) ▲
- Index cards (for mobiles) ▲
- String (for mobiles) ▲
- Item bucket (a large container of different types and sizes of an item)
- Circle graph activity (Situation Graph, p. 105)

Special Notes on the Use of These Menus

These menus mention the use of an item bucket for graphing. This bucket may contain different colors, sizes, or shapes of an item. Items that work well include buttons, counting bears, Unifix™ cubes, and even pencils.

Time Frame

- 1–2 weeks—Students are given the menus as the unit is started, and the teacher discusses all of the product options on the menu. As the different options are discussed, students will choose products that add to a total of 10 points. As the lessons progress through the week, the teacher and the students should refer back to the options associated with the content being taught.
- 1–2 days—The teacher chooses an activity from the menus to use with the entire class.

Suggested Forms

- All-purpose rubric
- Point-based free-choice proposal form

Using Graphs

Directions: Choose at least two activities from the menu below. The activities must total at least 10 points. Place a check mark next to each box to show which activities you will complete. All activities must be completed by:_____.

2 Points

- ❒ Create a mobile that shows the different types of graphs. Include a real-life example of each.
- ❒ Create a poster that shows all of the different types of graphs. Include a real-life example of each graph, tell the benefits of the graph, and explain when the graph should be used to show data.

5 Points

- ❒ Using a newspaper, locate three different graphs. Write a brief summary of what each graph is showing.
- ❒ Using the item bucket, create a graph that represents the bucket's contents.
- ❒ Create a children's book that shows readers about the different types of graphs and how they can be helpful to children.
- ❒ Free choice—Prepare a proposal form and submit it to your teacher for approval.

8 Points

- ❒ Design a survey to obtain your classmates' answers to a question. Present your information on a poster using a circle graph.
- ❒ Given the circle graph (Situation Graph, p. 105), write a story that could match the data.

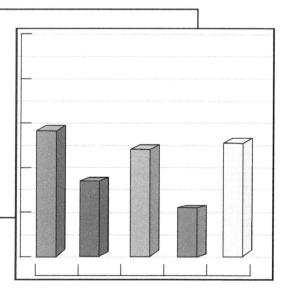

Name: _____

Using Graphs

Directions: Choose at least two activities from the menu below. The activities must total at least 10 points. Place a check mark next to each box to show which activities you will complete. All activities must be completed by:_____.

---

2 Points

❑ Using a newspaper, locate three different graphs. Write a brief summary of what each graph is showing.

❑ Create a poster that shows all of the different types of graphs. Include a real-life example of each graph, tell the benefits of the graph, and explain when it should be used to show data.

---

5 Points

❑ Design a survey to obtain your classmates' answers to a question. Present your information on a poster using a bar graph.

❑ Using the item bucket, create a circle graph that represents the bucket's contents.

❑ Create a children's book that shows readers about the different types of graphs and how they can be helpful to children.

❑ Free choice—Prepare a proposal form and submit it to your teacher for approval.

---

8 Points

❑ Select a science experiment whose data would be represented on a line graph. Conduct the experiment, record the data in a table, and draw your graph. Be sure that your teacher approves the experiment before you begin!

❑ Given the circle graph (Situation Graph, p. 105), write a story that could match the data.

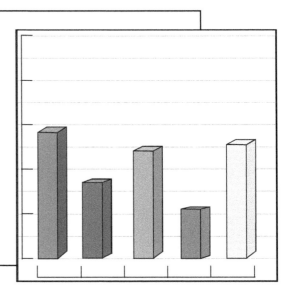

Situation Graph

Examine the circle graph below and develop a situation that
could match this graph. Be creative!

Mean, Median, and Mode

2-5-8 Menus

Objectives Covered Through These Menus and These Activities

- Students will calculate the mean, median, and mode of data.
- Students will understand the real-world applications of mean, median, and mode.

Materials Needed by Students for Completion

- Poster board or large white paper ▲
- Microsoft PowerPoint or other slideshow software ●
- Sports section of the newspaper
- Dice
- Large index cards (for instruction cards) ▲

Special Notes on the Use of These Menus

One menu option asks students to roll a die 100 times. If more than one student selects this option, the classroom may get rather noisy. Instead of using small, plastic dice, a cube template can be used to create paper dice, or large foam dice can be found at discount stores. Both of these options keep the sound at a reasonable level.

Time Frame

- 1–2 weeks—Students are given the menus as the unit is started, and the teacher discusses all of the product options on the menus. As the different options are discussed, students will choose products that add to a total of 10 points. As the lessons progress through the week, the teacher and the students should refer back to the options associated with the content being taught.
- 1–2 days—The teacher chooses an activity from the menus to use with the entire class.

Suggested Forms

- All-purpose rubric
- Point-based free-choice proposal form
- Student presentation rubric

Name:_____

Mean, Median, and Mode

Directions: Choose at least two activities from the menu below. The activities must total at least 10 points. Place a check mark next to each box to show which activities you will complete. All activities must be completed by:_____.

2 Points

- ❏ Create an instruction card that shows how to find the mean, median, and mode of data. Include at least one real-world example.
- ❏ Make a brochure that explains mean, median, and mode. It should explain how to find each and what each tells about the data.

5 Points

- ❏ Are dice really random? Record a hypothesis about what patterns will happen if you roll a set of dice 100 times. Roll the dice and record your data. Find the mean, median, and mode for your data.
- ❏ Create a questionnaire to gather data from three questions. Have at least 7 people complete your questionnaire. Present the mean, mode, and median of your data.
- ❏ Perform a song or rap that shares examples of mean, mode, and median and ways to remember the differences between each one.
- ❏ Free choice—Submit a free-choice proposal form to your teacher for approval.

8 Points

- ❏ Using the sports section of the newspaper, research the statistics of at least 15 players in one sport. After gathering the data, record the mean, median, and mode for the players. Explain what each number means to the sport.
- ❏ Are you the mean, mode, or median in your classroom? Choose one physical aspect of your classmates (e.g., height, head diameter, length of hands) and record the measurements for your classmates. Then, show the mean, median, and mode of your gathered information on a poster.

Mean, Median, and Mode

Directions: Choose at least two activities from the menu below. The activities must total at least 10 points. Place a check mark next to each box to show which activities you will complete. All activities must be completed by: _____.

2 Points

☐ Create a PowerPoint presentation that shows how to find the mean, median, and mode of data. Include at least one real-world example.

☐ Make a brochure that explains mean, median, and mode. You should explain how to find each and what each tells about the data.

5 Points

☐ Using the sports section of the newspaper, research the statistics of at least 15 players in one sport. After gathering the data, record the mean, median, and mode for the players. Explain what each number means to the sport.

☐ Are dice really random? Record a hypothesis about what patterns will happen if you roll a set of dice 100 times. Roll the dice and record your data. Find the mean, median, and mode for your data.

☐ Create a questionnaire to gather data from three questions. Have at least 10 people complete your questionnaire. Present the mean, mode, and median of your data.

☐ Free choice—Submit a free-choice proposal form to your teacher for approval.

8 Points

☐ What is the fairest way to calculate your grades for this class? Should teachers use the mean, median, or mode? Prepare a speech that explains which method is the most fair and why you believe this.

☐ Are you the mean, mode, or median in your classroom? Choose one physical aspect of your classmates (e.g., height, head diameter, length of hands) and record the measurements for your classmates. Then, show the mean, median, and mode of your gathered information.

Chapter 8

Geometry

 DOI: 10.4324/9781003234241-8

Lines and Congruency

2-5-8 Menus

Objectives Covered Through These Menus and These Activities

- Students will distinguish between perpendicular, parallel, and intersecting lines.
- Students will share the properties of perpendicular and parallel lines in real-world situations.
- Students will identify congruent shapes.

Materials Needed by Students for Completion

- Graph paper or Internet access (for crossword puzzles)
- Materials for student-created artwork (colored pencils, large paper, etc.)
- Magazines (with pictures of buildings)
- Shoe boxes (for dioramas) ▲
- Scrapbooking materials ▲
- Coat hangers (for mobiles)
- Index cards (for mobiles)
- String (for mobiles)
- Information on M. C. Escher

Time Frame

- 1–2 weeks—Students are given the menus as the unit is started, and the teacher discusses all of the product options on the menus. As the different options are discussed, students will choose products that add to a total of 10 points. As the lessons progress through the week, the teacher and the students should refer back to the options associated with the content being taught.
- 1–2 days—The teacher chooses an activity from the menus to use with the entire class.

Suggested Forms

- All-purpose rubric
- Point-based free-choice proposal form

Lines and Congruency

Directions: Choose at least two activities from the menu below. The activities must total at least 10 points. Place a check mark next to each box to show which activities you will complete. All activities must be completed by:_____.

2 Points

☐ Create a worksheet to quiz your classmates on the differences between parallel, perpendicular, and intersecting lines, as well as on how to tell if two figures are congruent.

☐ Make a mobile that shows examples of parallel, perpendicular, and intersecting lines.

5 Points

☐ Collect at least 10 photos from magazines that show both parallel and perpendicular lines. Create a collage or folder with these photos. Mark each set of parallel or perpendicular lines.

☐ Do you prefer parallel or perpendicular lines? Create a parallel or perpendicular scrapbook based on which you prefer. The scrapbook should be filled with objects you see on a daily basis. Tell about each object and why you prefer it.

☐ Make a crossword puzzle with parallel and perpendicular items as the clues.

☐ Free choice—Prepare a proposal form and submit it to your teacher for approval.

8 Points

☐ Create a diorama of a place on another planet in which things are only parallel to one another and there are no perpendicular lines at all.

☐ M. C. Escher was an artist who had many interesting styles. One of his techniques used congruent figures to create new and different patterns. Research this type of artwork and create a sample of your own based on Escher's method.

Name:_____

Lines and Congruency

Directions: Choose at least two activities from the menu below. The activities must total at least 10 points. Place a check mark next to each box to show which activities you will complete. All activities must be completed by:_____.

2 Points
- ☐ Create a worksheet to quiz your classmates on the differences between parallel, perpendicular, and intersecting lines, as well as on how to tell if two figures are congruent.
- ☐ Make a mobile that shows examples of parallel, perpendicular, and intersecting lines.

5 Points
- ☐ Collect 10 photos from magazines that show parallel and perpendicular lines. Create a collage or folder with these photos. Mark each set of parallel or perpendicular lines.
- ☐ When designing a building, using congruent pieces is sometimes very important. Collect pictures of buildings from magazines that were built using congruent or incongruent parts. Label each part and tell how that part impacted the structure.
- ☐ Make a crossword puzzle with parallel and perpendicular items as the clues.
- ☐ Free choice—Prepare a proposal form and submit it to your teacher for approval.

8 Points
- ☐ Certain letters have parallel parts. For example, the word "parallel" has parallel letters in it. Make a children's book of perpendicular and parallel objects that are spelled with perpendicular and parallel letters.
- ☐ M. C. Escher was an artist who had many interesting styles. One of his techniques used congruent figures to create new and different patterns. Research this type of artwork and create a sample of your own based on Escher's method.

Circles

2-5-8 Menus

Objectives Covered Through These Menus and These Activities
- Students will calculate the radius, diameter, and circumference of a circle.
- Students will understand the relationship between the measurements of radius and circumference.
- Students will use properties of a circle to solve real-world problems.

Materials Needed by Students for Completion
- Poster board or large white paper
- Art supplies (colored pencils, construction paper, etc.)
- Meter sticks or tape measures (for measuring room diameter)
- Magazines (for collages)
- Video camera (for news reports)
- Microsoft PowerPoint or other slideshow software

Special Notes on the Use of These Menus
Be sure you have enough meter sticks for the classroom measurement activity. Students really like being able to apply their knowledge to real-world situations, and having students measure the classroom to calculate the diameter can be distracting if class time is not planned for activity work.

Time Frame
- 1–2 weeks—Students are given the menus as the unit is started, and the teacher discusses all of the product options on the menus. As the different options are discussed, students will choose products that add to a total of 10 points. As the lessons progress through the week, the teacher and the students should refer back to the options associated with the content being taught.
- 1–2 days—The teacher chooses an activity from the menus to use with the entire class.

Suggested Forms
- All-purpose rubric
- Point-based free-choice proposal form ●
- Student presentation rubric

Circles

Directions: Choose at least two activities from the menu below. The activities must total at least 10 points. Place a check mark next to each box to show which activities you will complete. All activities must be completed by:_____.

2 Points

☐ Create a worksheet for your classmates about calculating the radius, diameter, and circumference of a circle.

☐ Create a collage of circular objects. Record the radius, diameter, and circumference for each object.

5 Points

☐ Create a song or rap to help you remember the different parts of a circle.

☐ Create an artistic masterpiece on a piece of paper. Your piece of art must contain at least three different-sized circles, at least four different colors, and only circles whose circumferences are larger than 20 cm but smaller than 50 cm.

☐ Circles are often used in sports. Create a PowerPoint presentation that shows their importance and includes at least five examples of how circles are used in sports.

☐ There are ways to find the circumference of a circle without calculating it using the radius. Create a flipbook that shows at least four ways you can find a circle's circumference without knowing the radius.

8 Points

☐ Your teacher would like to buy the largest circular rug possible to cover your classroom floor. Circular rugs are sold by diameter. Make a poster to propose to your teacher the size of rug that should be purchased. Include a drawing of the pattern and colors you think would be best.

☐ A crime has been committed! Create a news report in which the circumference of a circle helps to solve the crime.

Name: _____

Circles

Directions: Choose at least two activities from the menu below. The activities must total at least 10 points. Place a check mark next to each box to show which activities you will complete. All activities must be completed by:_____.

2 Points
- ☐ Create a worksheet for your classmates about calculating the radius, diameter, and circumference of a circle.
- ☐ Create a collage of circular objects. Record the radius, diameter, and circumference for each object.

5 Points
- ☐ Create a song or rap to help you remember the different parts of a circle.
- ☐ Your teacher would like to buy the largest circular rug possible to cover your classroom floor. Circular rugs are sold by diameter. Make a poster to propose to your teacher the size of rug that should be purchased. Include a drawing of the pattern and colors you think would be best.
- ☐ Circles are often used in sports. Create a PowerPoint presentation that shows their importance and at least five examples of how circles are used in sports.
- ☐ Free choice—Prepare a proposal form and submit it to your teacher for approval.

8 Points
- ☐ Create an artistic masterpiece on a poster board. Your piece of art must contain at least four different-sized circles, at least five different colors, and only circles whose circumference is larger than 20 cm but smaller than 50 cm. Be creative and provide an answer key on the back that proves that all of your circles meet these circumference criteria.
- ☐ A crime has been committed! Create a news report in which the circumference of a circle helps to solve the crime.

Geometric Shapes

Three Shape Menu ▲ and Tic-Tac-Toe Menu ●

Objectives Covered Through These Menus and These Activities
- Students will identify lines of symmetry in everyday objects.
- Students will name and identify various geometric shapes and solids.
- Students will identify the number of vertices, faces, and edges on geometric figures.
- Students will calculate area, perimeter, and volume of various geometric shapes.

Materials Needed by Students for Completion
- Poster board or large white paper
- Video camera (optional for videos) ●
- Materials for measuring shapes (rulers, measuring tapes, etc.)
- Magazines (for symmetry pictures)
- Blank index cards (for trading cards)
- Shoe boxes (for dioramas) ●
- Coat hangers (for mobiles) ▲
- Index cards (for mobiles) ▲
- String (for mobiles) ▲
- Scrapbooking materials ▲
- Materials for bedroom models ●
- Cube template

Special Notes on the Use of These Menus
This topic has two different menu formats: Three Shape menu and Tic-Tac-Toe menu. The Three Shape menu is specifically selected for the triangle (lower level) option, as it easily allows the menu to be broken into manageable bits. The menu itself can be cut into strips of the same shape. Students can then be given a strip of square product choices for their use. Once they have chosen and submitted the square product for grading, they can be given the circle strip, and lastly, they can complete the diamond strip. Because this type of menu is designed to become more advanced as students move through the shapes, teachers may choose to provide their students who have special needs with the top two shapes and save the diamonds for enrichment.

Time Frame

- 2 weeks—Students are given the menus as the unit is started. The teacher will go over all of the options for that content and have students note the activities they are most interested in completing. As the teacher presents lessons throughout the week, he or she should refer back to the options associated with that content. If students are using the Tic-Tac-Toe menu form, completed products should make a column or a row. If students are using the Three Shape menu form, they should complete one product from each different shape group. When students complete these patterns, they will have completed one activity from three different objectives, learning styles, or levels of Bloom's Revised taxonomy. When students complete the activities in this way, they will have completed one activity from each content area: lines of symmetry, naming and describing geometric shapes and solids, and measuring geometric shapes and solids.
- 1 week—At the start of the unit, the teacher chooses the three activities he or she feels are most valuable for the students. Stations can be set up in the classroom. These three activities are available for student choice throughout the week, as regular instruction takes place.
- 1–2 days—The teacher chooses an activity from the menus to use with the entire class.

Suggested Forms

- All-purpose rubric
- Free-choice proposal form ●

Name: _____

▲

Geometric Shapes

Directions: Choose one activity from each shape group. Circle one choice from each group of shapes. Color in the shape after you have finished it. All activities must be completed by: _____.

Cut 10 pictures from a magazine of objects with exactly one line of symmetry. Present your pictures on a poster with the line of symmetry carefully marked on each object.

Create a drawing of a nature scene in which each object in your drawing has exactly two lines of symmetry. Be creative in your drawing!

Living things have different kinds of symmetry. Research the different kinds and make a mobile to share examples of them.

Create a set of trading cards for all of the geometric shapes and solids. Include the number of vertices, faces, and edges for each.

Complete a cube with one geometric shape or solid on each side. For each shape, give a real-world example, as well as the number of vertices, faces, and edges.

Create a scrapbook for one of the geometric solids. The scrapbook should include examples, as well as this geometric solid's impact on our daily lives.

Complete a Venn diagram to compare and contrast area and perimeter. Include examples!

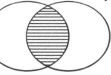

Find household examples of eight different shapes and solids. Measure each one, and in a chart, record the perimeters, areas, and volumes of the objects.

You want to fill your class-room with popcorn as a practical joke. Take measurements of the room and figure out a way to calculate how much popcorn would fit in the classroom!

119

Geometric Shapes

Directions: Check the boxes you plan to complete. They should form a tic-tac-toe across or down. All products are due by: _____.

☐ *Showing Symmetry* Using a magazine, cut out 10 pictures of objects that have exactly one line of symmetry. Present your pictures on a poster with the line of symmetry carefully marked on each.	☐ *Measuring Shapes* Complete a Venn diagram to compare and contrast area and perimeter. Include examples!	☐ *Naming and Describing Shapes* Create a model or diorama of your bedroom using examples of the geometric shapes. Create a key that tells the shapes that make up each object, as well as the number of vertices, faces, and edges for each.
☐ *Naming and Describing Shapes* Create a set of trading cards for all of the geometric shapes and solids. Include the number of vertices, faces, and edges for each.	☐ **Free Choice** (Fill out your proposal form before beginning the free choice!)	☐ *Measuring Shapes* Find household examples of eight different shapes and solids. Measure each one, and in a chart, record its perimeter, area, and volume.
☐ *Measuring Shapes* Many artists use the lines of geometric forms in their work. Make an artistic video about vertices, edges, and faces that we see every day.	☐ *Naming and Describing Shapes* Complete a cube with one geometric shape or solid on each side. Give a real-world example of each shape, as well as the number of vertices, faces, and edges for each.	☐ *Showing Symmetry* Create a drawing of a nature scene in which each object in your drawing has exactly two lines of symmetry. Be creative in your drawing!

Geometric Shapes Cube

Complete the cube for geometric shapes. Place one geometric shape or solid on each side. Give a real-world example of the shape, as well as the number of vertices, faces, and edges for each. Use this pattern or create your own cube.

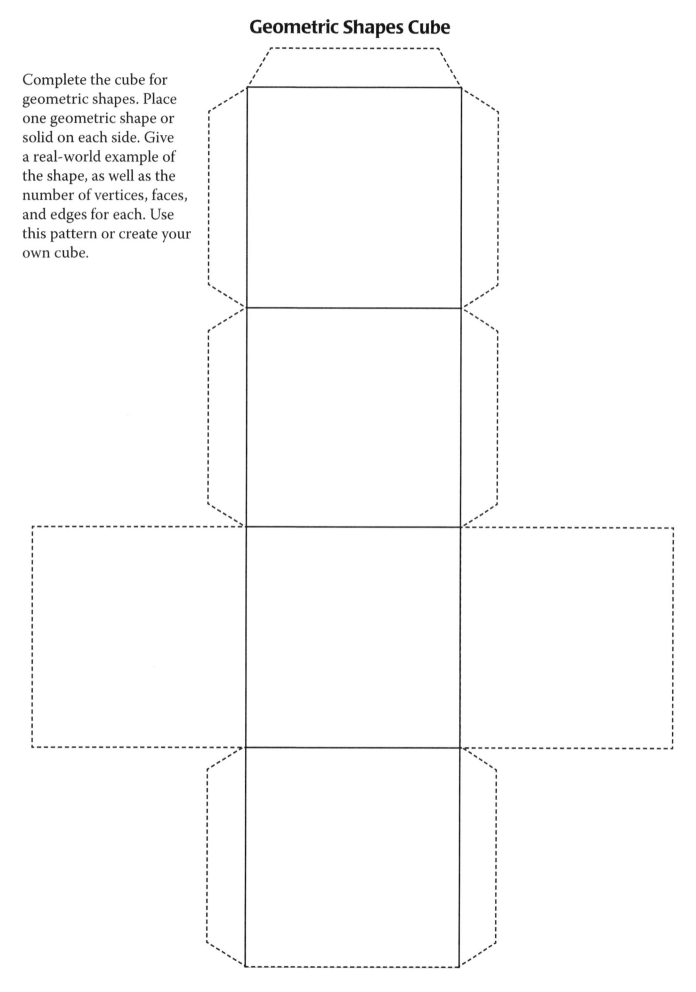

CHAPTER 9

Measurement

 DOI: 10.4324/9781003234241-9

Measuring Capacity

Three Shape Menu ▲ and Tic-Tac-Toe Menu ●

Objectives Covered Through These Menus and These Activities

- Students will use milliliters, liters, cups, pints, and gallons to measure capacity.
- Students will estimate capacity using both standard and metric units.
- Students will solve real-world problems in both standard and metric units.

Materials Needed by Students for Completion

- Poster board or large white paper
- Newspapers
- Metric measuring lab
- Gallon Person activity (p. 128)
- Video camera (for commercials)
- Blank index cards (for concentration cards) ▲
- Materials for board games (folders, colored cards, etc.) ▲
- Cube template ●

Special Notes on the Use of These Menus

This topic has two different menu formats: Three Shape menu and Tic-Tac-Toe menu. The Three Shape menu is specifically selected for the triangle (lower level) option, as it easily allows the menu to be broken into manageable bits. The menu itself can be cut into strips of the same shape. Students can then be given a strip of square product choices for their use. Once they have chosen and submitted the square product for grading, they can be given the circle strip, and lastly, they can complete the diamond strip. Because this type of menu is designed to become more advanced as students move through the shapes, teachers may choose to provide their students who have special needs with the top two shapes and save the diamonds for enrichment.

Time Frame

- 2 weeks—Students are given the menus as the unit is started. The teacher will go over all of the options for that content and have students note the activities they are most interested in completing. As the teacher presents lessons throughout the week, he or she should refer back to the options associated with that content. If students are using the Tic-Tac-Toe menu form, completed products should make a column or a row. If students are using the Three Shape menu form, they should complete one product from each different shape group. When students complete these patterns, they will have completed one activity from three different objectives, learning styles, or levels of Bloom's Revised taxonomy. When students complete activities in this way, they will have completed one activity from each content area: metric units of capacity, standard units of capacity, and capacity in the real world.

- 1 week—At the start of the unit, the teacher chooses the three activities he or she feels are most valuable for the students. Stations can be set up in the classroom. These three activities are available for student choice throughout the week, as regular instruction takes place.
- 1–2 days—The teacher chooses an activity from the menus to use with the entire class.

Suggested Forms

- All-purpose rubric
- Free-choice proposal form ●
- Student presentation rubric

▲

Measuring Capacity

Directions: Choose one activity from each shape group. Circle one choice from each group of shapes. Color in the shape after you have finished it. All activities must be completed by: _____.

Create a flipbook for milliliters, liters, cups, pints, gallons, and quarts. On each page, create a math problem that involves that unit. The problem should be realistic.

Search through a newspaper to find articles or advertisements that use units of capacity. Create a poster collage that shows all of your examples.

Design a set of concentration cards for matching units of capacity with examples that are measured in those units. Be sure to include an answer key!

Create a capacity collection. Collect two household items that are measured in each unit: cups, pints, quarts, and gallons. This will give you a total of eight items to bring to class.

Create a poster showing the gallon person. Make each part of the body out of an item that would be measured in the unit shown.

Create a song about estimating and measuring using cups, pints, quarts, and gallons. Include examples in your song.

The Smiths are buying a pool for their back-yard (20 yards wide and 30 yards deep). Pools are sized in liters. Research pool sizes and calculate how many liters the largest possible pool would hold.

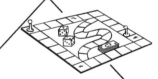

Create a commercial for a warehouse that stocks products in large quantities. The commercial will air in a country that uses the metric system, so your examples will need to be metric.

Create a board game in which players practice using kiloliters, liters, and milliliters.

Name: _____

Measuring Capacity

Directions: Check the boxes you plan to complete. They should form a tic-tac-toe across or down. All products are due by: _____.

☐ *Capacity in Our World* Create a flipbook for each unit of capacity: milliliters, liters, cups, pints, gallons, and quarts. On each page, create a math problem that involves that unit. The problem should be realistic.	☐ *Metric Units* Create a commercial for a warehouse store that only carries large quantities of its products. This commercial is going to air in a country that uses the metric system, so all of your examples will need to be metric.	☐ *Standard Units* Create a poster using the gallon person as a model. Create each part of the body out of items that would be measured in the corresponding unit.
☐ *Standard Units* Create a capacity collection. Collect two household items that are measured in each unit: cups, pints, quarts, and gallons. This will give you a total of eight items to bring to class.	☐ **Free Choice** (Fill out your proposal form before beginning the free choice!)	☐ *Metric Units* Create two metric capacity cubes. You will create a liter cube and a milliliter cube. For the sides of the cubes, you will need to draw or locate pictures or examples of different metric capacities requested.
☐ *Metric Units* Your neighbors are purchasing a new pool. Their backyard is quite large (20 yards wide and 30 yards deep). Unfortunately, the pool dealer will only deal in pools sized in liters. Research pool sizes and decide on the largest number of liters their pool could hold based on the size of their backyard.	☐ *Standard Units* Create a song about estimating and measuring using cups, pints, quarts, and gallons. Include examples in your song.	☐ *Capacity in Our World* Search through a newspaper to find articles or advertisements that use units of capacity. Create a poster collage that shows all of your examples. 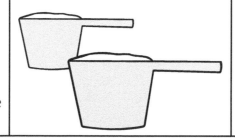

Gallon Person

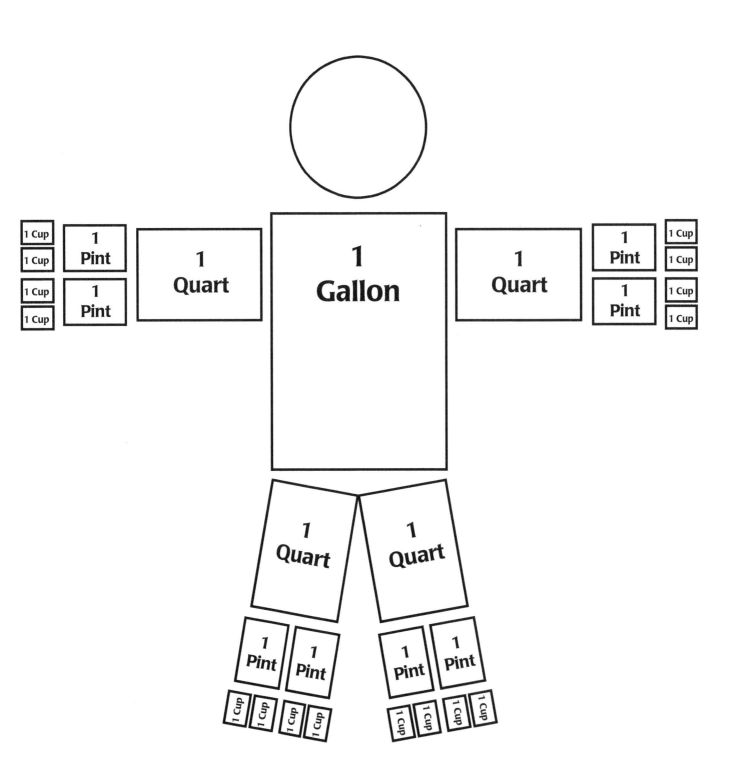

Metric Liter Capacity Cube

Each side of this cube should have a picture or drawing of an item that has the approximate liter capacity indicated. Use this pattern or create your own cube.

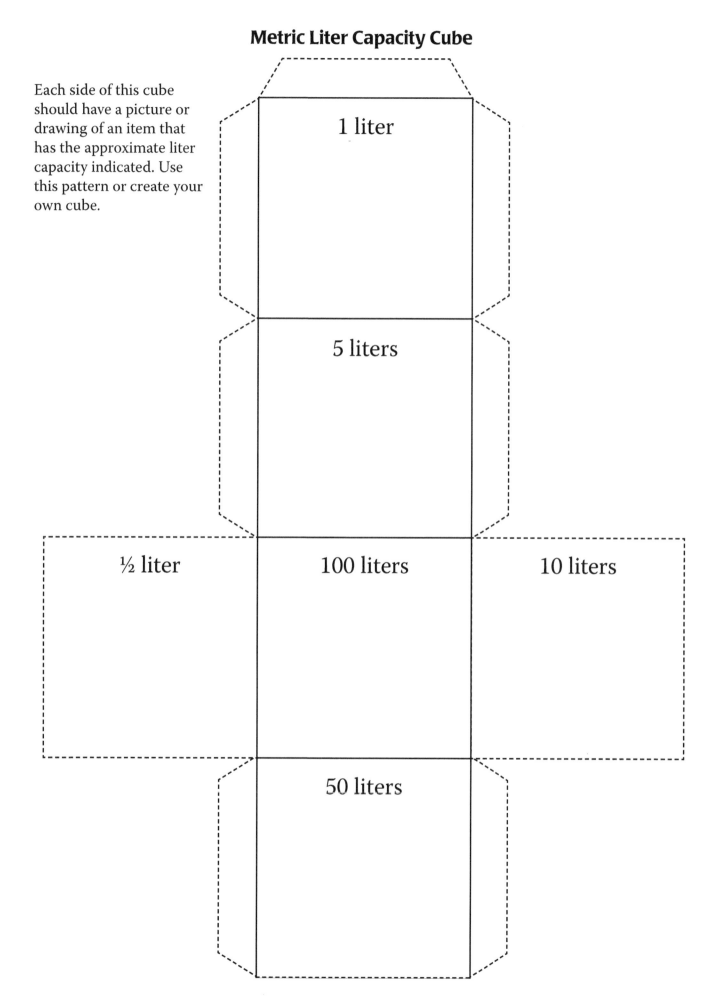

1 liter

5 liters

½ liter

100 liters

10 liters

50 liters

Metric Milliliter Capacity Cube

Each side of this cube should have a picture or drawing of an item that has the approximate milliliter capacity indicated. Use this pattern or create your own cube.

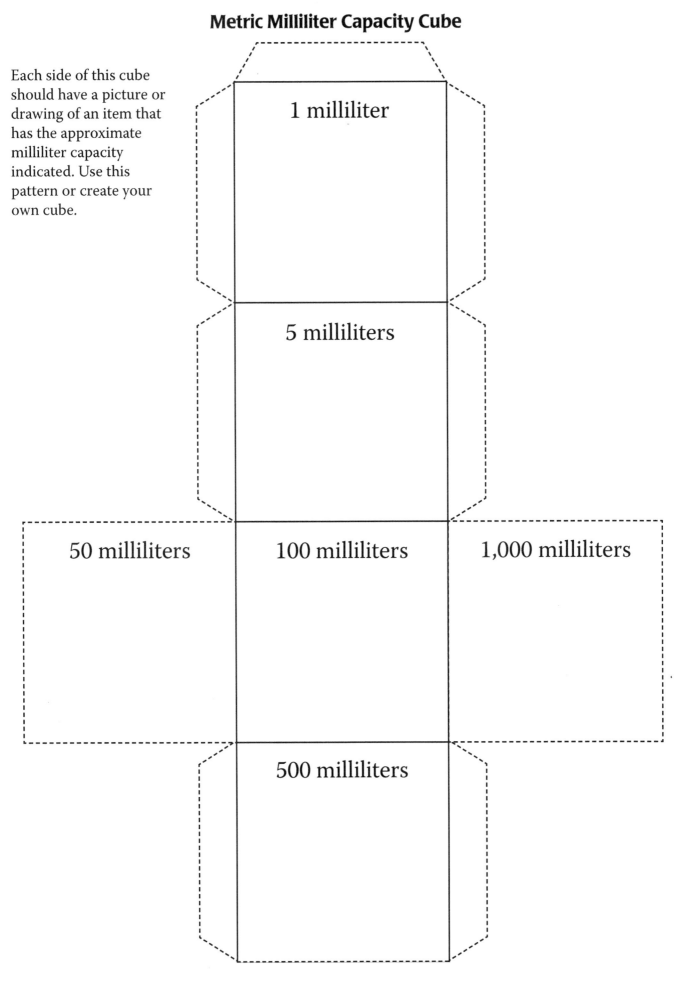

1 milliliter

5 milliliters

50 milliliters   100 milliliters   1,000 milliliters

500 milliliters

Time

Three Shape Menu ▲ and Tic-Tac-Toe Menu ●

Objectives Covered Through These Menus and These Activities
- Students will explain the importance of telling time.
- Students will solve real-world problems using time and schedules.

Materials Needed by Students for Completion
- Poster board or large white paper
- Microsoft PowerPoint or other slideshow software
- Blank index cards (for concentration card games)
- Page from newspaper with daily movie times
- Access to the Internet and airline websites
- School schedule activity (p. 135)
- Video camera (for commercials) ●
- Digital or analog watches ▲

Special Notes on the Use of These Menus
One of the options on the triangle (lower level) menu asks students to wear a watch if they do not normally wear one. Students may not have watches at home, so it is always helpful if the teacher has a few extra working watches. These might be donated to the classroom at the beginning of the school year, or they can be acquired fairly inexpensively at thrift stores.

These menus allow the students to create their own race around the country. This works best when students have access to maps and different airline websites. The students can choose the date for their "race" and see what flights can be found. This is a time-intensive activity because there are so many options available.

This topic has two different menu formats: Three Shape menu and Tic-Tac-Toe menu. The Three Shape menu is specifically selected for the triangle (lower level) option, as it easily allows the menu to be broken into manageable bits. The menu itself can be cut into strips of the same shape. Students can then be given a strip of square product choices for their use. Once they have chosen and submitted the square product for grading, they can be given the circle strip, and lastly, they can complete the diamond strip. Because this type of menu is designed to become more advanced as students move through the shapes, teachers may choose to provide their students who have special needs with the top two shapes and save the diamonds for enrichment.

Time Frame

- 2 weeks—Students are given the menus as the unit is started. The teacher will go over all of the options for that content and have students note the activities they are most interested in completing. As the teacher presents lessons throughout the week, he or she should refer back to the options associated with that content. If students are using the Tic-Tac-Toe menu form, completed products should make a column or a row. If students are using the Three Shape menu form, they should complete one product from each different shape group. When students complete these patterns, they will have completed one activity from three different objectives, learning styles, or levels of Bloom's Revised taxonomy.
- 1 week—At the start of the unit, the teacher chooses the three activities he or she feels are most valuable for the students. Stations can be set up in the classroom. These three activities are available for student choice throughout the week, as regular instruction takes place.
- 1–2 days—The teacher chooses an activity from the menus to use with the entire class.

Suggested Forms

- All-purpose rubric
- Free-choice proposal form ●
- Student presentation rubric

Time

Directions: Choose one activity from each shape group. Circle one choice from each group of shapes. Color in the shape after you have finished it. All activities must be completed by: _____.

Create a poster that explains how to read both a digital and an analog clock.

Create a concentration game for both digital and analog clocks and the time they tell.

Perform your own song about how to tell time. It should include examples of both digital and analog clocks. You may use a clock while singing the song to demonstrate.

Some people think that students do not need to learn to read an analog clock. Do you agree? Why or why not? Prepare a pamphlet that shows your point of view.

There are many time zones around the world (even in the U.S.). Prepare a PowerPoint presentation that describes the reason for time zones and why their locations are defined as they are.

If you always wear a watch, take it off for 2 days. If you do not wear a watch, wear one for 2 days. Based on your experience, create an advertisement to promote wearing or not wearing a watch.

Thinking about all of the components that go into creating a schedule, complete the Create Your Own School Schedule activity.

You are racing across the U.S. to visit three major cities of your choice. Research airline schedules online and prepare an itinerary showing the fastest route for visiting the three cities.

Analyze current movie times and create a schedule that allows you to see as many movies as possible within the day. You cannot leave one movie in the middle to go to another.

Name: _____

Time

Directions: Check the boxes you plan to complete. They should form a tic-tac-toe across or down. All products are due by: _____.

☐ *Do You Know Time?* Create a poster that explains how to read both a digital and an analog clock.	☐ *Are You in the Zone?* There are many time zones around the world (even in the United States). Prepare a PowerPoint presentation that describes the reason for time zones and why their locations are defined as they are.	☐ *Can You Balance Time?* Thinking about all of the components that go into creating a schedule, complete the Create Your Own School Schedule activity.
☐ *Can You Go Around the World?* You are participating in a race across the United states, visiting at least five major cities of your choice. Using the Internet to find the schedules of major airlines, prepare an itinerary that shows the fastest route for visiting all five cities.	☐ **Free Choice** (Fill out your proposal form before beginning the free choice!)	☐ *Is Analog Outdated?* A group of students would like our state to change its policy on learning how to tell time. They don't think that students need to learn anything except how to read a digital clock. Do you agree? Why or why not? Prepare a pamphlet that shows your point of view.
☐ *Is Time Important?* People refer to analog clocks in many ways other than just telling time (for example, to indicate direction). Create a commercial for the analog clock and its various uses other than telling time.	☐ *Are You the Best Couch Potato?* A movie theater is holding a daylong movie marathon for just $10. Analyze current movie times and create a schedule that allows you to see as many movies as possible within the day. You cannot leave one movie in the middle to go to another.	☐ *Do You Have the Time?* Create a concentration game for both digital and analog clocks and the time they tell.

Name: _____

Create Your Own School Schedule

You have been presented with the task of creating a workable schedule for the students in your grade level. Here is what you will need to consider:

- Students must spend at least 45 minutes a day on each subject area.
- Students must have at least 30 minutes a day for lunch.
- Students must have at least 45 minutes each day for elective time (e.g., physical education, music, library).
- Your school day should start and finish at the same times it does now.

Using these guidelines, design the perfect weekly schedule for your classmates. You may be creative in rotating the elective classes each day and allowing recess or extra time during lunches as time allows. Make a presentation of your schedule on a large poster board. Include the advantages and disadvantages of your schedule.

Use the chart below to brainstorm your ideas.

Times	Monday	Tuesday	Wednesday	Thursday	Friday

What are the advantages and disadvantages to your plan? _____

_____

_____

Measuring Length

2-5-8 Menus

Objectives Covered Through These Menus and These Activities
- Students will use centimeters, meters, inches, feet, and yards to measure length.
- Students will estimate length using both standard and metric units.
- Students will use both standard and metric units to address real-world situations.

Materials Needed by Students for Completion
- Poster board or large white paper
- Length scavenger hunt activity (p. 139)
- Cube template ▲
- Tools for measuring (meter sticks, rulers, etc.)
- Coat hangers (for mobiles)
- Index cards (for mobiles)
- String (for mobiles)
- Microsoft PowerPoint or other slideshow software
- Newspapers

Time Frame
- 1–2 weeks—Students are given the menus as the unit is started, and the teacher discusses all of the product options on the menus. As the different options are discussed, students will choose products that add to a total of 10 points. As the lessons progress through the week, the teacher and the students should refer back to the options associated with the content being taught.
- 1–2 days—The teacher chooses an activity from the menus to use with the entire class.

Suggested Forms
- All-purpose rubric
- Point-based free-choice proposal form

Measuring Length

Directions: Choose at least two activities from the menu below. The activities must total at least 10 points. Place a check mark next to each box to show which activities you will complete. All activities must be completed by:_____.

2 Points

- ❏ Create a mobile with the different units for measuring length. For each unit, include an example of an object that would best be measured with that unit.
- ❏ Go through the newspaper to locate articles that give examples of length. Prepare a poster with at least eight examples.

5 Points

- ❏ Create a cube with a different length on each side, and measure items in your classroom or school that have different lengths. Find two items for each side of the cube to match the target measurement.
- ❏ Design a PowerPoint presentation that shows how to choose the proper units for measuring different lengths. Include information on how to properly measure length.
- ❏ Create a folded quiz book in which users estimate and then measure the lengths of target items. Be sure to double check your answers!
- ❏ Free choice—Prepare a proposal form and submit it to your teacher for approval.

8 Points

- ❏ Create a map of your school. (You may have to do some measuring!) Develop a scale for your map using appropriate units.
- ❏ Complete the Length Scavenger Hunt activity.

Name: _____

Measuring Length

Directions: Choose at least two activities from the menu below. The activities must total at least 10 points. Place a check mark next to each box to show which activities you will complete. All activities must be completed by:_____.

2 Points

- ❏ Create a mobile with the different units for measuring length. For each unit, include an example of an object that would be best measured with that unit.
- ❏ Go through the newspaper to locate articles that give examples of length. Prepare a poster with at least eight examples.

5 Points

- ❏ Complete the Length Scavenger Hunt activity.
- ❏ Design a PowerPoint presentation that shows how to choose the proper units for measuring lengths. Include information on how to properly measure length.
- ❏ Create a folded quiz book in which users estimate and then measure the lengths of target items. Be sure to double check your answers!
- ❏ Free choice—Prepare a proposal form and submit it to your teacher for approval.

8 Points

- ❏ Create a map of your school. (You may have to do some measuring!) Develop a scale for your map using appropriate units.
- ❏ Choose a large item in the classroom that you could rebuild using wood. After measuring all of the parts of the item, write instructions that tell how you could make the item. Include a parts list and exact measurements in your instructions.

Name: _____

Length Scavenger Hunt

Your goal is to find items in your classroom (or school) that match each of the following lengths. For each length:

1. Choose an item.
2. Record its name under the First Guess column.
3. Measure the item or distance (e.g., from the door to my desk).
4. Is it within one unit of the target length? If so, go on to the next length. If not, try another item.

You only get two tries to find an item, so choose carefully!

Target Length	First Guess Item or Distance	Actual Length	Within One? (circle)	Second Guess Item or Distance	Actual Length	Within One? (circle)
1 cm			Y N			Y N
3 cm			Y N			Y N
10 cm			Y N			Y N
40 cm			Y N			Y N
1 m			Y N			Y N
1.5 m			Y N			Y N
3 m			Y N			Y N
10 m			Y N			Y N
1 in.			Y N			Y N
3 in.			Y N			Y N
8 in.			Y N			Y N
1 ft			Y N			Y N
2 ft			Y N			Y N
1 yd			Y N			Y N
5 yd			Y N			Y N

Length Cube

Measure the items in your classroom or school. On each side, record or draw at least two items that have the given length. Use this pattern or create your own cube.

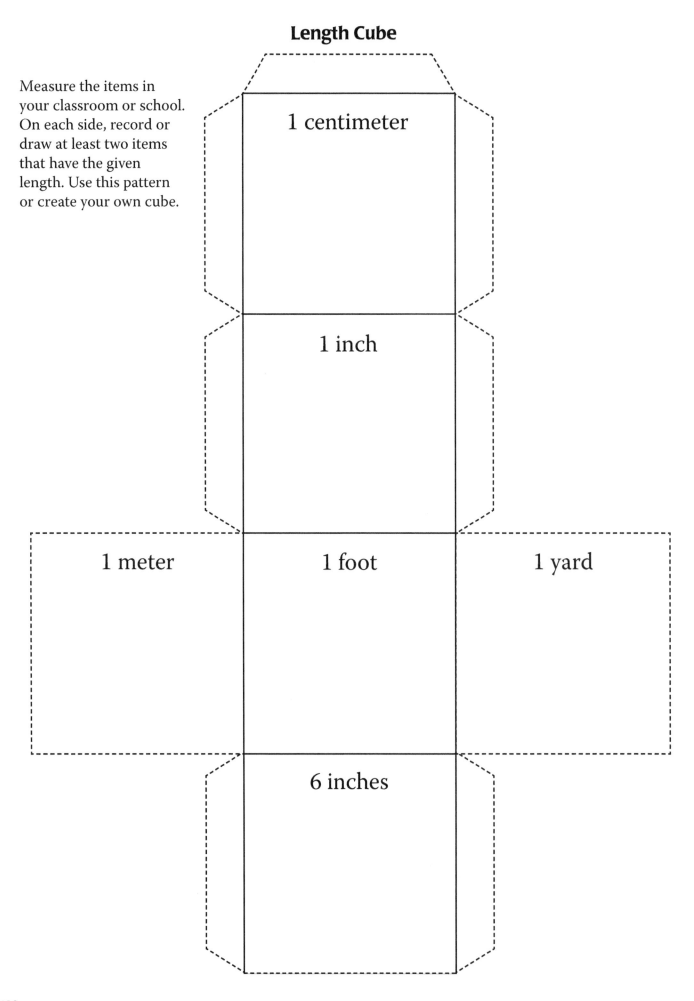

1 centimeter

1 inch

1 meter   1 foot   1 yard

6 inches

Measuring Temperature

Three Shape Menu ▲ and Tic-Tac-Toe Menu ●

Objectives Covered Through These Menus and These Activities
- Students will use thermometers to measure temperature.
- Students will estimate temperature.
- Students will solve real-world problems using temperature.

Materials Needed by Students for Completion
- Poster board or large white paper
- Graph paper (for graphing temperature)
- Newspapers
- Blank index cards (for trading cards)
- Large index cards (for instruction cards)
- Measuring temperature activity (p. 145)
- Cups (for measuring temperature activity)
- Graduated cylinder (for measuring temperature activity)
- Thermometers (for measuring temperature activity)
- Ice cubes (for measuring temperature activity)

Special Notes on the Use of These Menus

Although these menus do include an experiment, it involves relatively few supplies and can be set up as a station for the students. Students can either come to the station or take the supplies to their desks to complete this activity.

This topic has two different menu formats: Three Shape menu and Tic-Tac-Toe menu. The Three Shape menu is specifically selected for the triangle (lower level) option, as it easily allows the menu to be broken into manageable bits. The menu itself can be cut into strips of the same shape. Students can then be given a strip of square product choices for their use. Once they have chosen and submitted the square product for grading, they can be given the circle strip, and lastly, they can complete the diamond strip. Because this type of menu is designed to become more advanced as students move through the shapes, teachers may choose to provide their students who have special needs with the top two shapes and save the diamonds for enrichment.

Time Frame

- 2 weeks—Students are given the menus as the unit is started. The teacher will go over all of the options for that content and have students note the activities they are most interested in completing. As the teacher presents lessons throughout the week, he or she should refer back to the options associated with that content. If students are using the Tic-Tac-Toe menu form, completed products should make a column or a row. If students are using the Three Shape menu form, they should complete one product from each different shape group. When students complete these patterns, they will have completed one activity from three different objectives, learning styles, or levels of Bloom's Revised taxonomy. When students complete activities in this way, they will have completed one activity from each content area: estimating temperature, using temperature, and measuring temperature.
- 1 week—At the start of the unit, the teacher chooses the three activities he or she feels are most valuable for the students. Stations can be set up in the classroom. These three activities are available for student choice throughout the week, as regular instruction takes place.
- 1–2 days—The teacher chooses an activity from the menus to use with the entire class.

Suggested Forms

- All-purpose rubric
- Free-choice proposal form ●
- Student presentation rubric ▲

Measuring Temperature

Directions: Choose one activity from each shape group. Circle one choice from each group of shapes. Color in the shape after you have finished it. All activities must be completed by: _____.

Create a brochure to help other students your age better estimate temperature. Include specific examples and a quiz to test their abilities.

Create a set of trading cards for different temperatures to help you estimate temperatures better (e.g., boiling, freezing, warm enough for no coat).

Some people are great at estimating temperature. Interview a family member who is a good estimator about his or her talent and share the results with your classmates.

Complete the Measuring Temperature activity.

Create an instruction card showing how to measure temperature, including a drawing for each step. Follow your instructions to measure the temperature outside to be sure you haven't missed a step.

Measure the temperatures of two different locations in your school for a week. Record your data. Write a conclusion that shares your findings and explains any surprises.

Cut out the national temperature chart from the newspaper for a week. Choose three cities in different areas. Create a graph to show how the temperatures have changed throughout the week.

Create a children's book about temperature. The book should tell readers about different temperatures and how they may affect people's daily lives.

Certain household items and materials work best only at certain temperatures. Find five examples of these items. Prepare a poster that shows the items and how temperature affects them.

Name: _____

Measuring Temperature

Directions: Check the boxes you plan to complete. They should form a tic-tac-toe across or down. All products are due by: _____.

☐ *Estimating Temperature* Create a set of trading cards for different temperatures. These cards should help you estimate temperatures better, so choose your temperatures carefully (e.g., boiling, freezing, warm enough for no coat).	☐ *Measuring Temperature* Complete the Measuring Temperature activity.	☐ *Using Temperature* Cut out the national temperature chart in your newspaper for a week. Choose three cities in different parts of the United States. Create a graph to show how the temperature has changed throughout the week.
☐ *Using Temperature* Create a children's book about temperature. The book should tell readers about different temperatures and how they affect people's daily lives.	☐ **Free Choice** (Fill out your proposal form before beginning the free choice!)	☐ *Measuring Temperature* Create an instruction card that shows how to properly measure temperature. Include drawings of each step. Use your instruction card to measure the temperature outside to be sure you have not missed any steps.
☐ *Measuring Temperature* Using a thermometer, measure the temperature of two different locations in your school for a week. Create a data table to record your information. Write a conclusion that shares your findings and explains any surprises.	☐ *Using Temperature* Certain household items have temperature restrictions for their use. They work best only at certain temperatures. Find eight examples of these items. Prepare a poster that shows the items and how temperature affects them.	☐ *Estimating Temperature* Create a brochure to help other students your age better estimate temperature. Include specific examples and a quiz to test their abilities.

144

Name: _____

Measuring Temperature

Materials: four cups, water, ice cubes, thermometer

Procedure:
1. Put 100 ml of tap water into each cup.
2. Record the temperature of each cup. (They should be very close in temperature because they are from the same water source.)
3. Look at your data table and make some predictions about how you think ice cubes will change the temperature of the water. For each cup, fill in the temperature you think will result from the melting of the ice cubes.
4. In the first cup, place one ice cube.
5. In the second cup, place two ice cubes.
6. In the third cup, place three ice cubes.
7. In the fourth cup, place four ice cubes.
8. Allow the ice cubes to melt in each cup.
9. Measure the temperature in each cup and calculate how close your guesses were.
10. Empty your cups and clean up your area.

Data:

Cup	Temperature Without Ice	Your Prediction Temperature	Actual Temperature	Difference
1				
2				
3				
4				

Questions:
1. Using all of your information, how much temperature change will one ice cube make?

2. If you had to predict the temperature change for 10 ice cubes, what would you predict as the new temperature? Explain your reasoning.

Measuring Weight

Three Shape ▲ and Tic-Tac-Toe Menu ●

Objectives Covered Through These Menus and These Activities

- Students will measure weight in standard and metric units.
- Students will estimate weight using both standard and metric units.
- Students will solve real-world problems in both standard and metric units.

Materials Needed by Students for Completion

- Triple beam balances
- Blank index cards (for trading cards)
- Poster board or large white paper ●
- Bucket of items (various classroom items)
- Internet access for postage information (http://www.usps.com)

Special Notes on the Use of These Menus

This topic has two different menu formats: Three Shape menu and Tic-Tac-Toe menu. The Three Shape menu is specifically selected for the triangle (lower level) option, as it easily allows the menu to be broken into manageable bits. The menu itself can be cut into strips of the same shape. Students can then be given a strip of square product choices for their use. Once they have chosen and submitted the square product for grading, they can be given the circle strip, and lastly, they can complete the diamond strip. Because this type of menu is designed to become more advanced as students move through the shapes, teachers may choose to provide their students who have special needs with the top two shapes and save the diamonds for enrichment.

Time Frame

- 2 weeks—Students are given the menus as the unit is started. The teacher will go over all of the options for that content and have students note the activities they are most interested in completing. As the teacher presents lessons throughout the week, he or she should refer back to the options associated with that content. If students are using the Tic-Tac-Toe menu form, completed products should make a column or a row. If students are using the Three Shape menu form, they should complete one product from each different shape group. When students complete these patterns, they will have completed one activity from three different objectives, learning styles, or levels of Bloom's Revised taxonomy.

- 1 week—At the start of the unit, the teacher chooses the three activities he or she feels are most valuable for the students. Stations can be set up in the classroom. These three activities are available for student choice throughout the week, as regular instruction takes place.
- 1–2 days—The teacher chooses an activity from the menus to use with the entire class.

Suggested Forms

- All-purpose rubric
- Free-choice proposal form ●
- Student presentation rubric ●

Measuring Weight

Directions: Choose one activity from each shape group. Circle one choice from each group of shapes. Color in the shape after you have finished it. All activities must be completed by: _____.

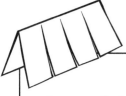

Create a flipbook for 1 ounce, 1 pound, 1 gram, and 1 kilogram. Inside each flap, draw at least three items that are close to these measurements.

Create a set of trading cards for milligram, gram, kilogram, ounce, pound, and ton. Include examples of items that represent those weights.

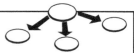

Create a weight mind map that includes all of the weight units as well as other ideas that come to mind for each.

Choose six items in your classroom that have different weights. After weighing each item, make a windowpane that shows the items from heaviest to lightest. Include the weight of each item.

Choose one unit of weight to investigate. Collect household objects that show one unit of that mass (e.g., objects that all weigh 1 pound). Bring your collection to school to share.

Using the bucket of items provided by your teacher, predict the items' weights in a data chart. Weigh the items and record their actual weights. Include one column to record how close your guesses were.

Elevators always have a weight limit for safety. If a small elevator can only hold 1,000 pounds, how many of your math books could the elevator carry at one time?

You want to send a book to your pen pal, who lives in a nearby state. The post office charges by weight. Weigh your book and determine how much it would cost to mail it.

You are taking a trip and can take only 29 pounds of luggage on the plane. List the items (and their weights) that you would take on a 2-week trip if your empty suitcase weighs 3 pounds.

Name: _____ ●

Measuring Weight

Directions: Check the boxes you plan to complete. They should form a tic-tac-toe across or down. All products are due by: _____.

☐ *How Much Is One?* Create a flipbook for 1 ounce, 1 pound, 1 gram, and 1 kilogram. Inside each flap, draw at least three items that are close to these vmeasurements.	☐ *Does It Carry Weight?* Elevators always have a weight limit for safety. If an elevator can only hold 2,000 pounds, how many of your math books could the elevator carry at one time?	☐ *Worth Reading?* You have decided that you want to share your favorite book with your pen pal, who lives in a nearby state. The post office charges by weight, so weigh your book and determine how much it would cost to send it to your pen pal.
☐ *Are They All the Same?* Some small items (such as paperclips) are sold by count, but they are packaged by weight so that the manufacturer avoids having to count out all of the items. Choose two products that are packaged based on weight rather than count and see how accurate the advertised count is. Make a poster of your results.	☐ **Free Choice** (Fill out your proposal form before beginning the free choice!)	☐ *What Does This Weight Look Like?* Choose one unit of weight you would like to investigate. Collect household objects that show one unit of that mass (e.g., objects that all weigh 1 pound). Bring your collection to school to share with your classmates.
☐ *Are You a Good Guesser?* Using the bucket of items provided by your teacher, predict the weight of each item. Create a data chart to record your predictions. Then weigh the items and record their actual weights. Include one column to record how close you were for each item.	☐ *Do You Know Your Weights?* Create a set of trading cards for milligram, gram, kilogram, ounce, pound, and ton. Include examples of items that represent those weights.	☐ *Could You Board?* The Fly by Night Airline has decided to limit the weight of passenger luggage. They have decided that every passenger can only take 29 pounds of luggage on any trip. You plan to travel for 2 weeks, and your empty suitcase weighs 3 pounds. List the items you would take on your trip and the weight of each.

References

Anderson, L., & Krathwohl, D. (Eds.). (2001). *A taxonomy for learning, teaching, and assessing: A revision of Bloom's taxonomy of educational objectives* (Complete ed.). New York, NY: Longman.

Keen, D. (2001). *Talent in the new millennium: Report on year one of the programme.* Retrieved from http://www.dce. ac.nz/research/content _talent.htm

Magner, L. (2000). Reaching all children through differentiated assessment: The 2-5-8 plan. *Gifted Child Today, 23*(3), 48–50.

Mercer, C. D., & Lane, H. B. (1996). Empowering teachers and students with instructional choices in inclusive settings. *Remedial & Special Education, 17,* 226–236.

Resources

Assouline, S. G., & Lupkowski-Shoplik, A. (2011). *Developing math talent: A comprehensive guide to math education for gifted students in elementary and middle school* (2nd ed.). Waco, TX: Prufrock Press.

Bollow, N., Berg, R., & Tyler, M. W. (2000). *Alien math*. Waco, TX: Prufrock Press.

Conway, J. H., & Guy, R. K. (1996). *The book of numbers*. New York, NY: Copernicus.

Fadiman, C. (1997). *The mathematical magpie*. New York, NY: Copernicus.

Field, A. (2004). *The great math experience: Engaging problems for middle school mathematics*. Victoria, BC: Trafford.

Kleiman, A., Washington, D., & Washington, M. F. (1996). *It's alive! Math like you've never known it before*. Waco, TX: Prufrock Press.

Kleiman, A., Washington, D., & Washington, M. F. (1996). *It's alive! And kicking!: Math the way it ought to be—tough, fun, and a little weird*. Waco, TX: Prufrock Press.

Lee, M., & Miller, M. (1999). *Real-life math investigations (grades 5–8)*. New York, NY: Scholastic.

Miller, M., & Lee, M. (2001). *40 fabulous math mysteries kids can't resist (grades 4–8)*. New York, NY: Scholastic.

Pappas, T. (2001). *The joy of mathematics: Discovering mathematics all around you*. San Carlos, CA: Wide World/Tetra.

Pappas, T. (2002). *Fractals, googols, and other mathematical tales.* San Carlos, CA: Wide World/Tetra.

Schwartz, D. M. (1998). *G is for googol: A math alphabet book.* Berkeley, CA: Tricycle Press.

Scieszka, J., & Smith, L. (1995). *Math curse.* New York, NY: Viking Books.

Tyler, M. W. (1995). *Real life math mysteries.* Waco, TX: Prufrock Press.

Zaccaro, E. (2003). *Primary grade challenge math.* Bellevue, IA: Hickory Grove Press.

Zaccaro, E. (2003). *The ten things all future mathematicians and scientists must know (but are rarely taught).* Bellevue, IA: Hickory Grove Press.

Zaccaro, E. (2005). *Challenge math for the elementary and middle school student (2nd ed.).* Bellevue, IA: Hickory Grove Press.

Zaccaro, E. (2006). *Becoming a problem solving genius.* Bellevue, IA: Hickory Grove Press.

About the Author

After teaching science for more than 15 years, both overseas and in the U.S., **Laurie E. Westphal** now works as an independent gifted education and science consultant nationwide. She enjoys developing and presenting staff development on differentiation for various districts and conferences, working with teachers to assist them in planning and developing lessons to meet the needs of all students. Laurie currently resides in Houston, TX, and has made it her goal to convert as many teachers as she can to the differentiated lifestyle in the classroom and share her vision for real-world, product-based lessons that help all students become critical thinkers and effective problem solvers.

If you are interested in having Laurie speak at your next staff development day or conference, please visit her website, http://www.giftedconsultant.com, for additional information.

Common Core State Standards Alignment

This book aligns with an extensive number of the Common Core State Standards in Math. Please visit http://www.routledge.com/ccss to download a complete packet of the standards that align with each indi-vidual menu in this book.

Additional Titles by the Author

Laurie E. Westphal has written many books on using differentiation strategies in the classroom, providing teachers of grades K–12 with creative, engaging, ready-to-use resources. Among them are:

 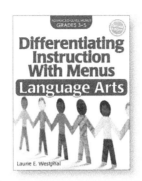  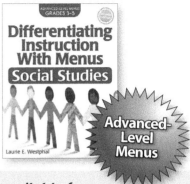

Math, Language Arts, Science, and Social Studies volumes available for:

Differentiating Instruction With Menus, Grades K–2

Differentiating Instruction With Menus, Grades 3–5, Second Edition

Differentiating Instruction With Menus, Grades 6–8, Second Edition

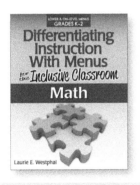 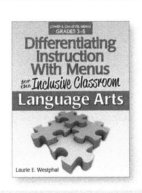  

Math, Language Arts, Science, and Social Studies volumes available for:

Differentiating Instruction With Menus for the Inclusive Classroom, Grades K–2

Differentiating Instruction With Menus for the Inclusive Classroom, Grades 3–5

Differentiating Instruction With Menus for the Inclusive Classroom, Grades 6–8

Literature for Every Learner, Grades 3–5; 6–8; and 9–12

Differentiating Instruction With Menus: Algebra I/II, Grades 9–12

Differentiating Instruction With Menus: Biology, Grades 9–12

For a current listing of Laurie's books, please visit Taylor & Francis **at http://www.routledge.com.**